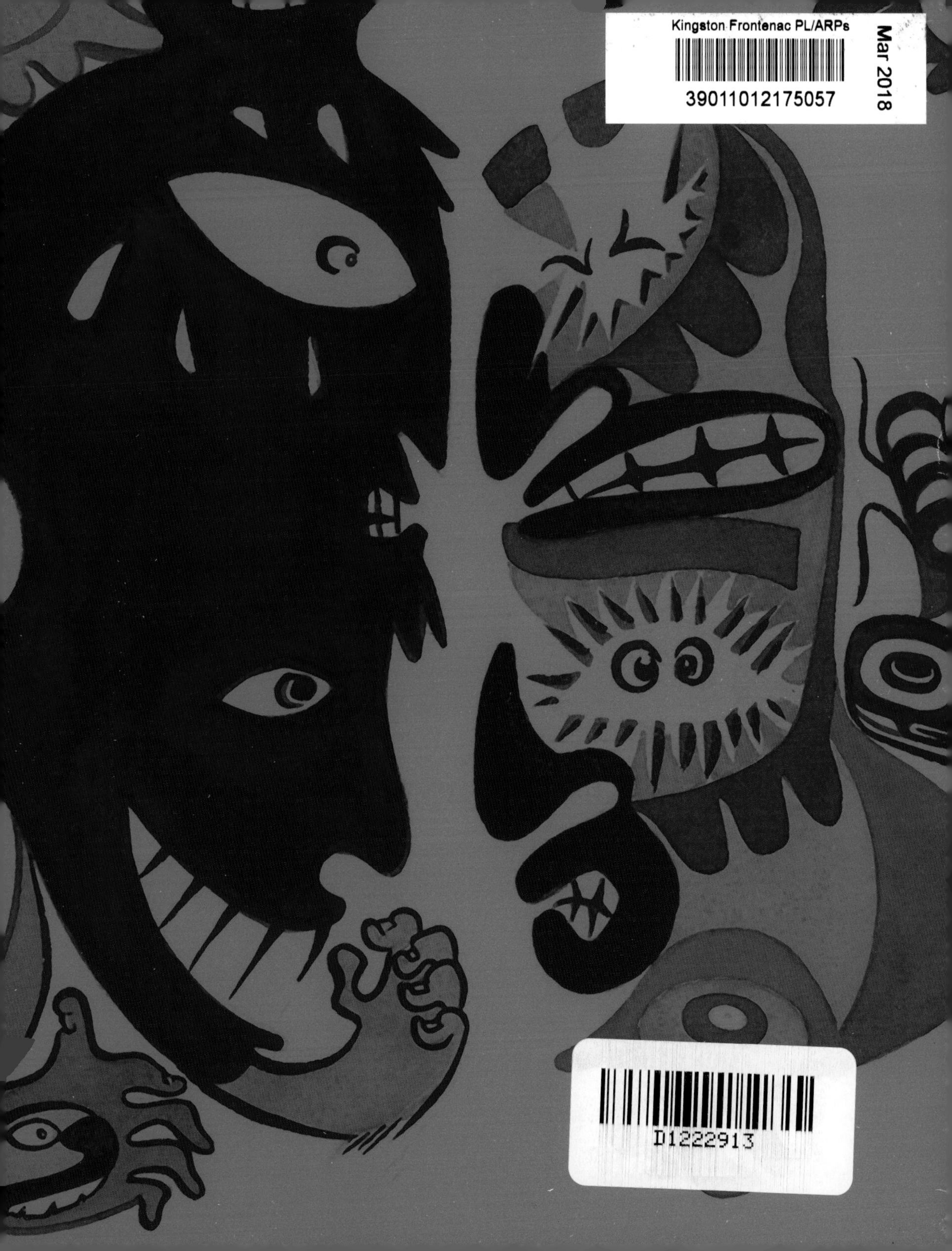

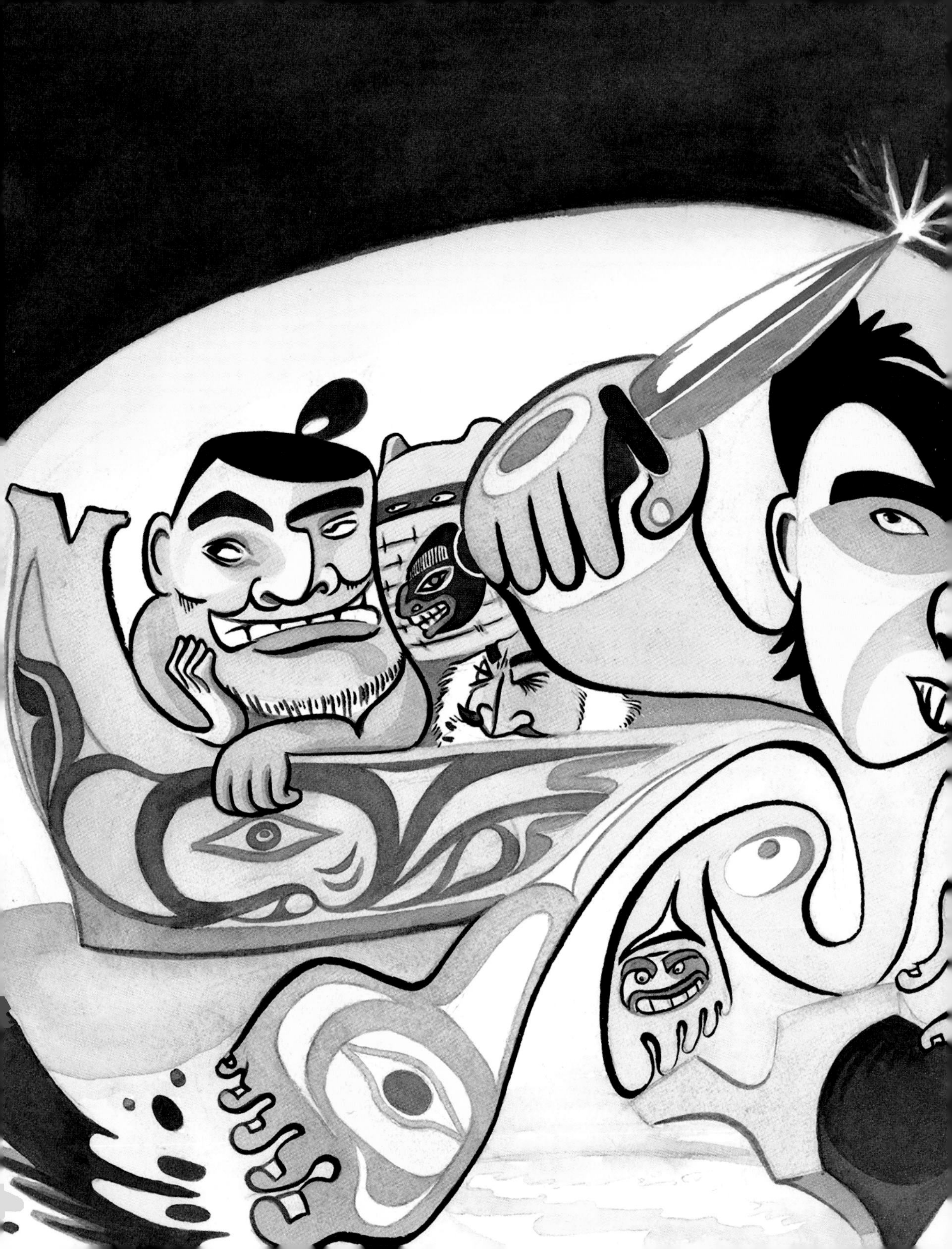

MICHAEL NICOLL
YAHGULANAAS

WAR OF THE BLINK

LOCARNO PRESS

An unusual series of events took place a few summers ago. Two groups of Indigenous Peoples from two separate nations on the North Pacific coast had dinner together. Not once but twice, in two towns in their two homelands.

It would not be a surprise if you hadn't heard of these events, as the reason for them took place long before there was a Canada or a United States. But it should not be a surprise that there are peoples who remember when there was no such thing as a Canada or a United States.

I grew gently older amongst my people. Our place is a most lovely and profoundly powerful archipelago where memories are not discarded but remain alive and are actively refreshed. We share memories with neighbouring Indigenous Peoples and their places.

This is a story of one such memory.

This is a story of war.

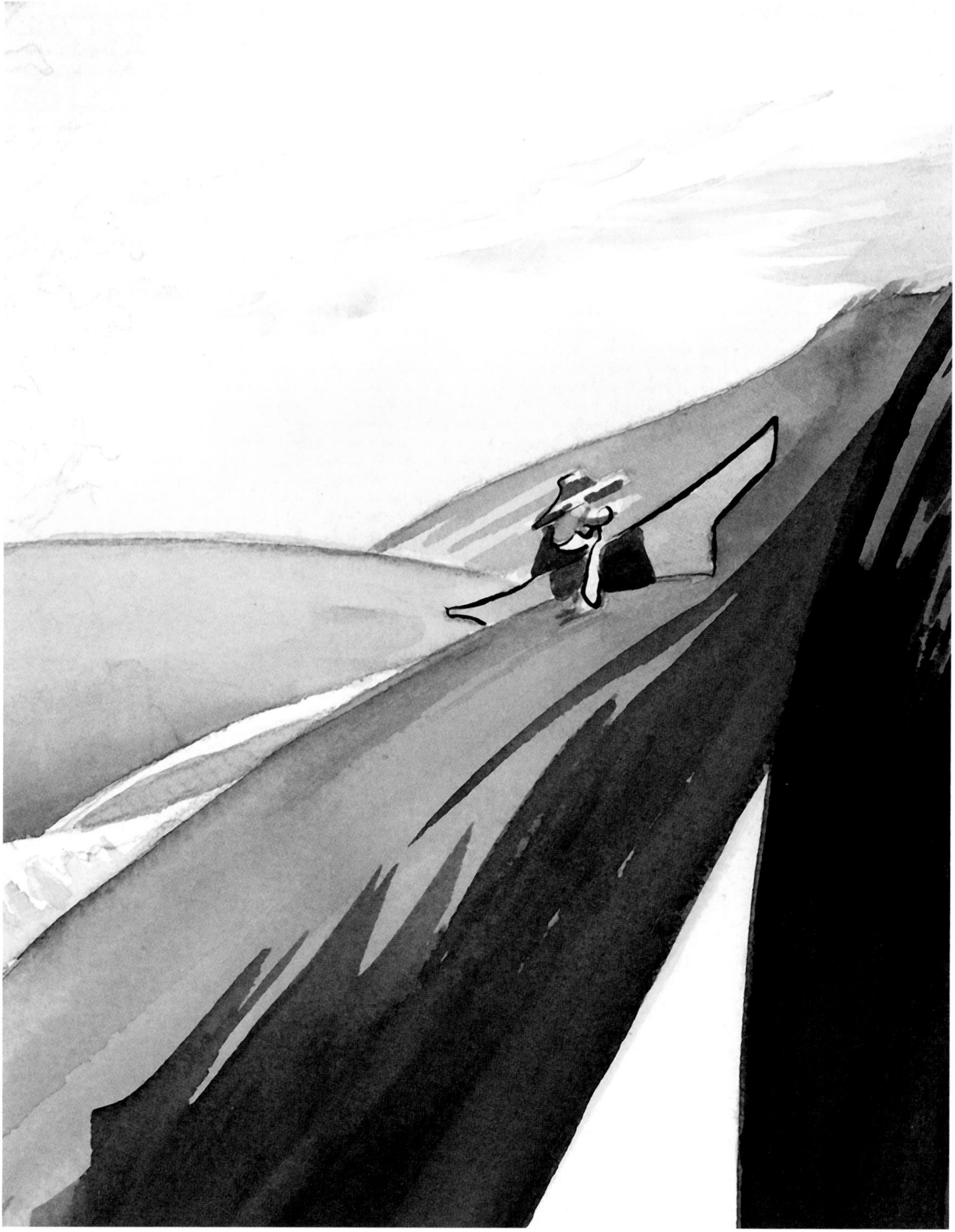

ONCE UPON A TIME,
THIS WAS A TRUE STORY...

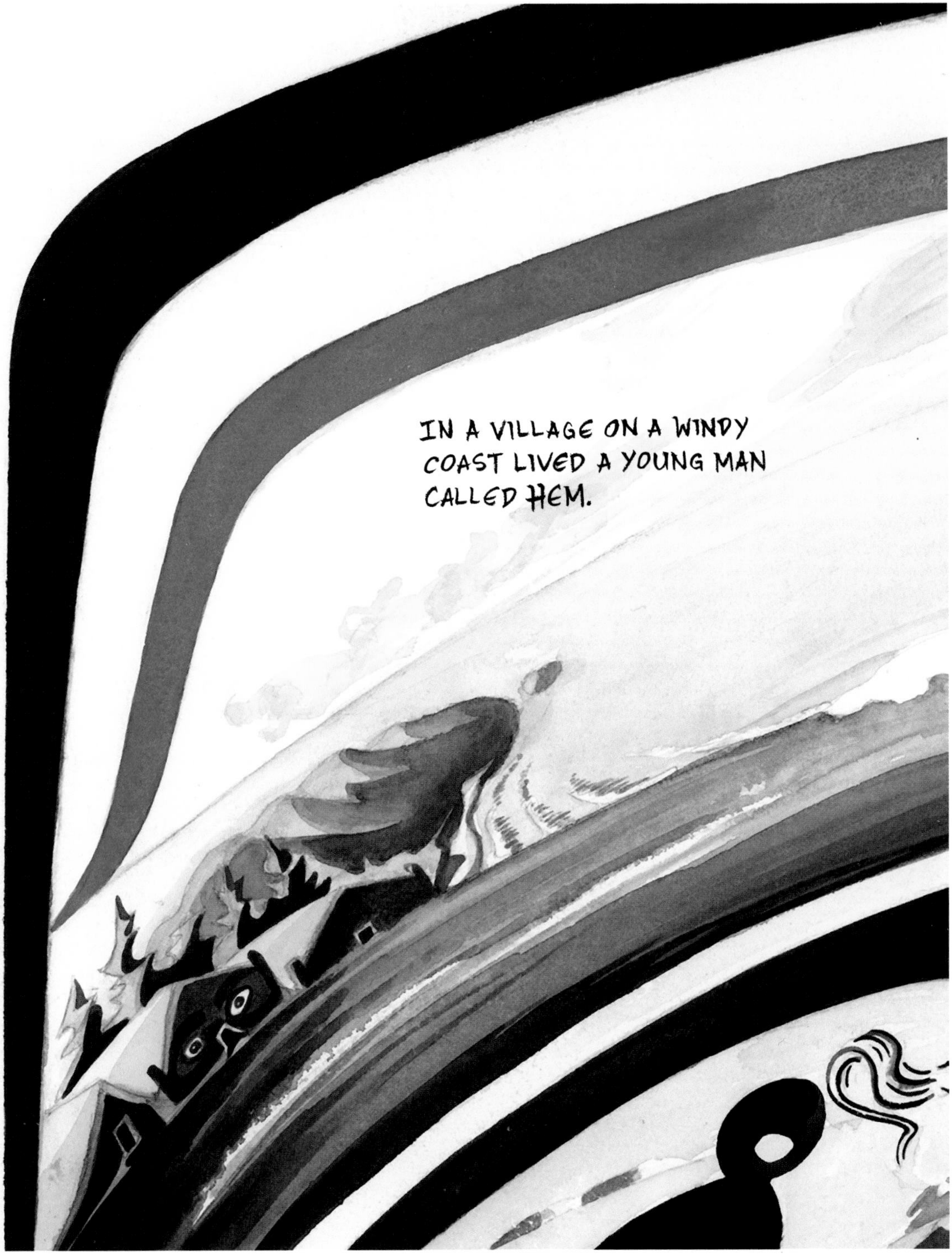
IN A VILLAGE ON A WINDY COAST LIVED A YOUNG MAN CALLED HEM.

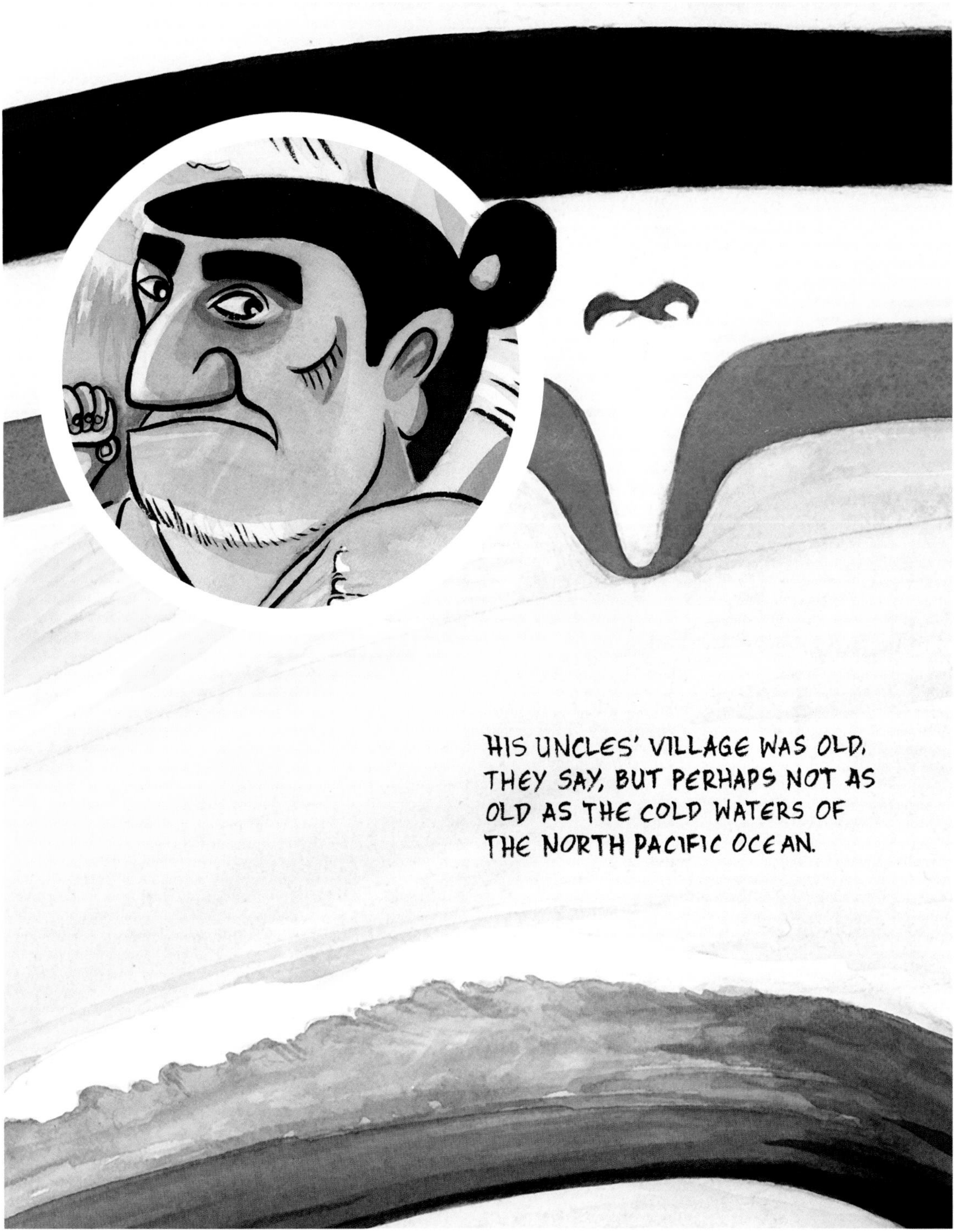
HIS UNCLES' VILLAGE WAS OLD, THEY SAY, BUT PERHAPS NOT AS OLD AS THE COLD WATERS OF THE NORTH PACIFIC OCEAN.

HEM HAD HEARD STORIES OF
AN ARCHIPELAGO THAT DRIFTED
JUST BEYOND THE HORIZON'S
RIM FAR OUT IN THE OCEAN.

BECAUSE THOSE ISLANDS
WERE ALWAYS ON THE EDGE OF
CONCEALMENT THEY WERE
CALLED XHAAYDLA GWAAYAAY.

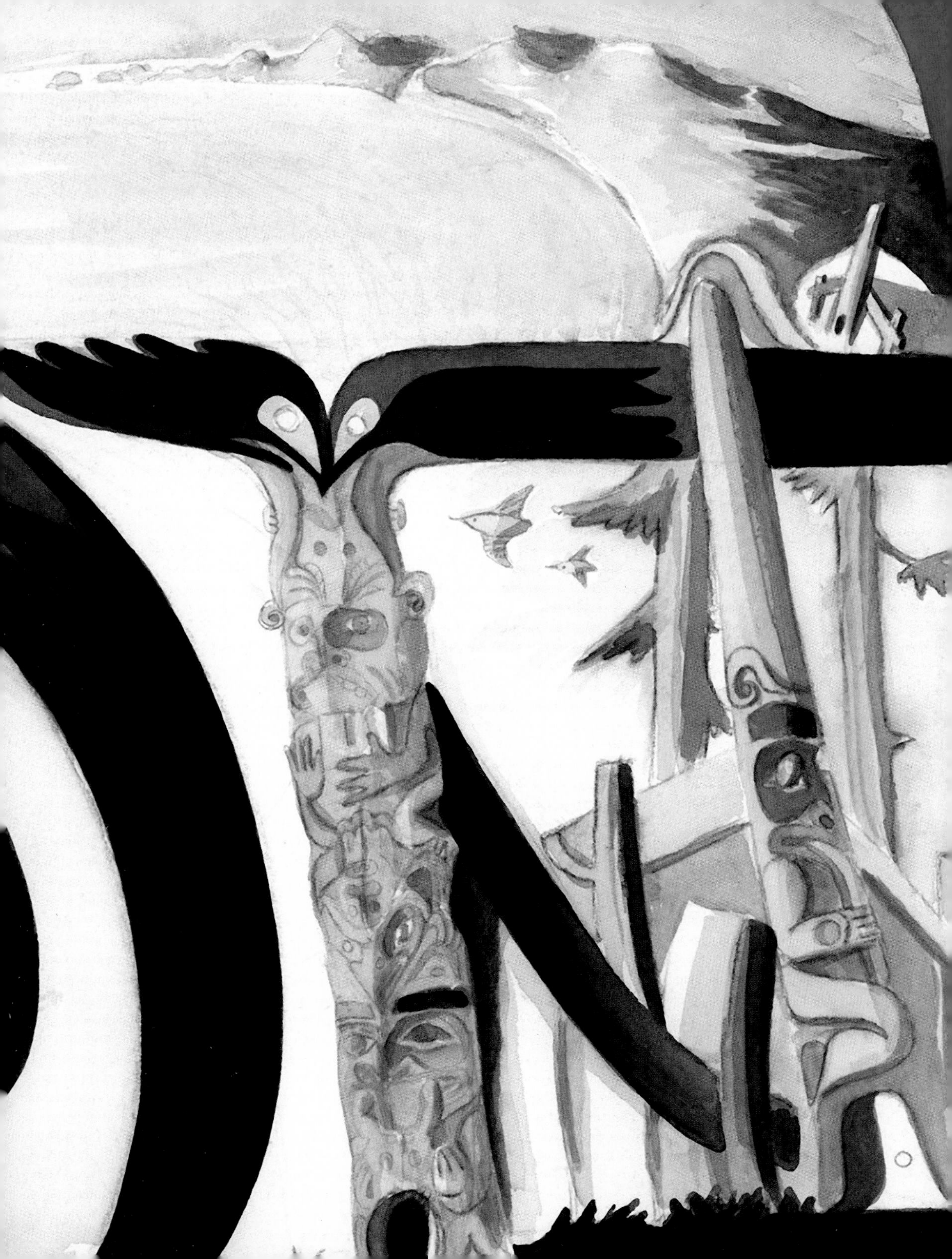

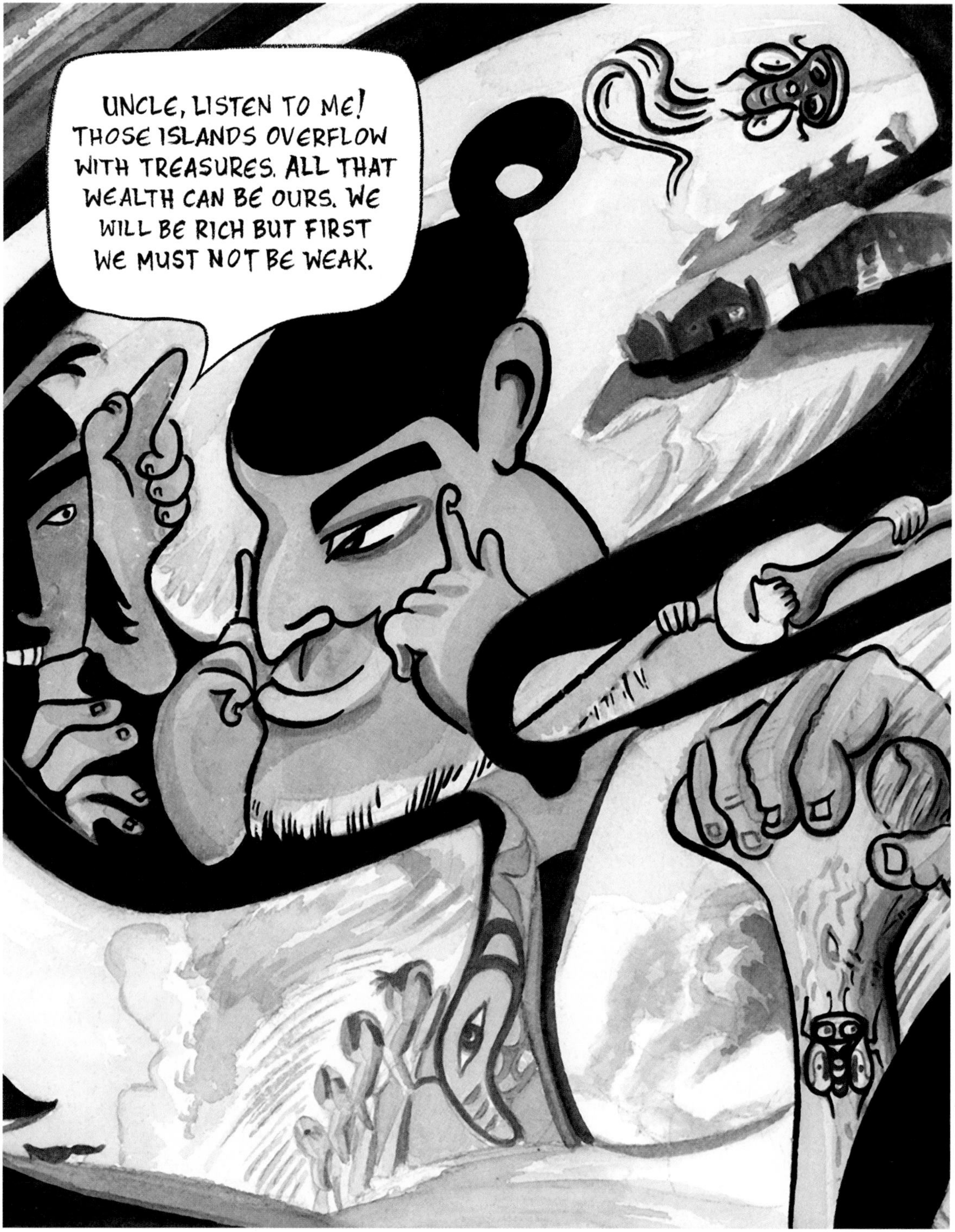
UNCLE, LISTEN TO ME! THOSE ISLANDS OVERFLOW WITH TREASURES. ALL THAT WEALTH CAN BE OURS. WE WILL BE RICH BUT FIRST WE MUST NOT BE WEAK.

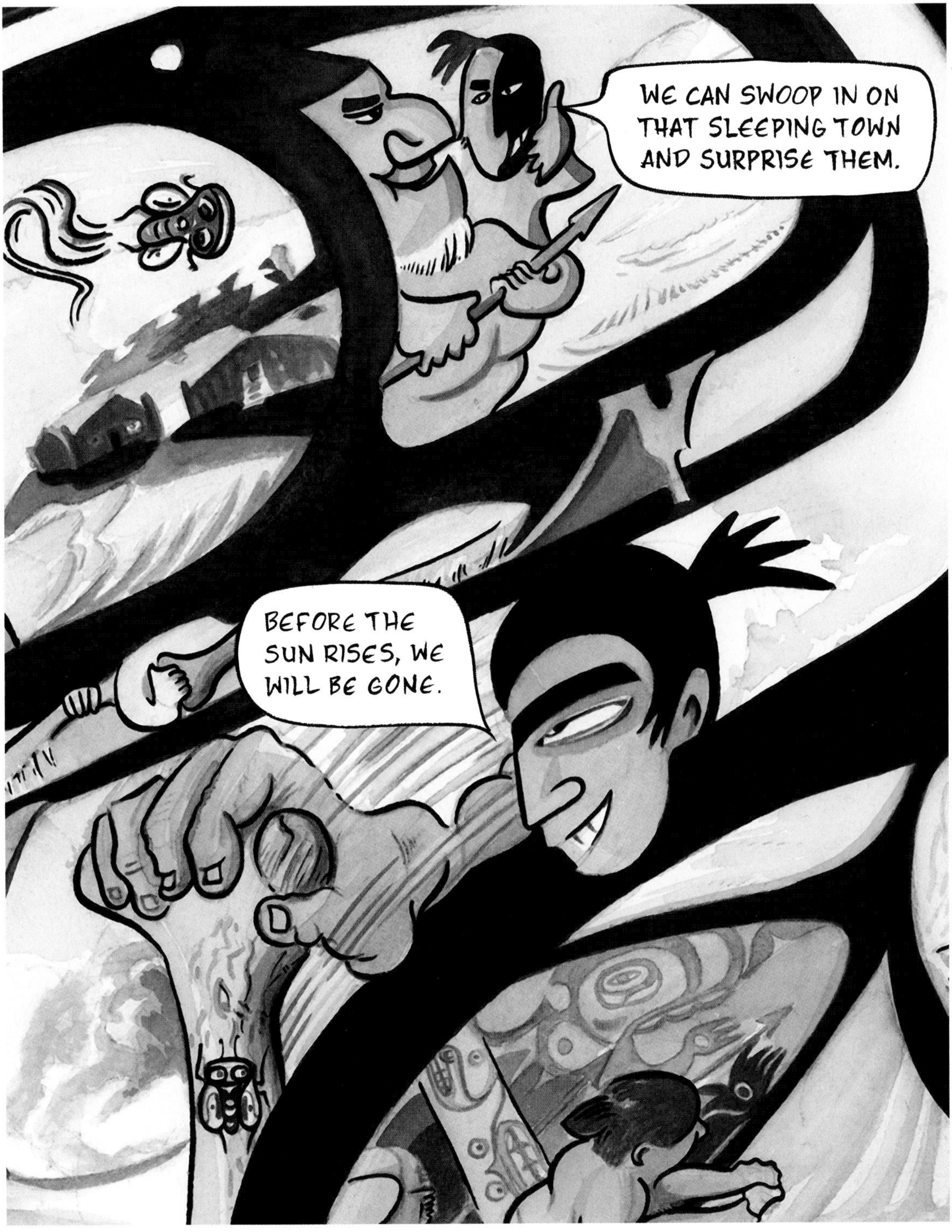
WE CAN SWOOP IN ON THAT SLEEPING TOWN AND SURPRISE THEM.
BEFORE THE SUN RISES, WE WILL BE GONE.

A FLY IN THE SKY SAW IT ALL,
THEY SAY

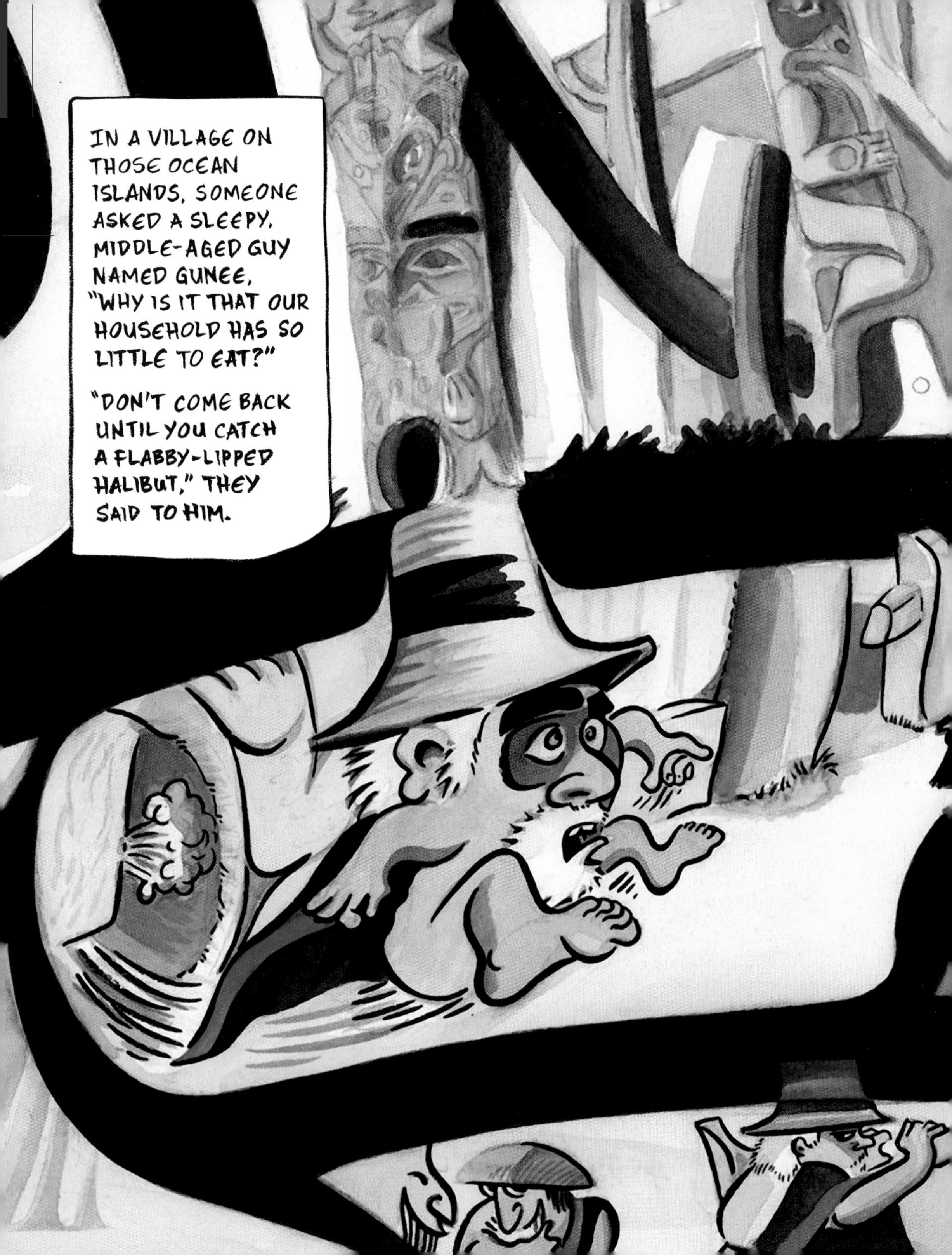
IN A VILLAGE ON THOSE OCEAN ISLANDS, SOMEONE ASKED A SLEEPY, MIDDLE-AGED GUY NAMED GUNEE, "WHY IS IT THAT OUR HOUSEHOLD HAS SO LITTLE TO EAT?"
"DON'T COME BACK UNTIL YOU CATCH A FLABBY-LIPPED HALIBUT," THEY SAID TO HIM.

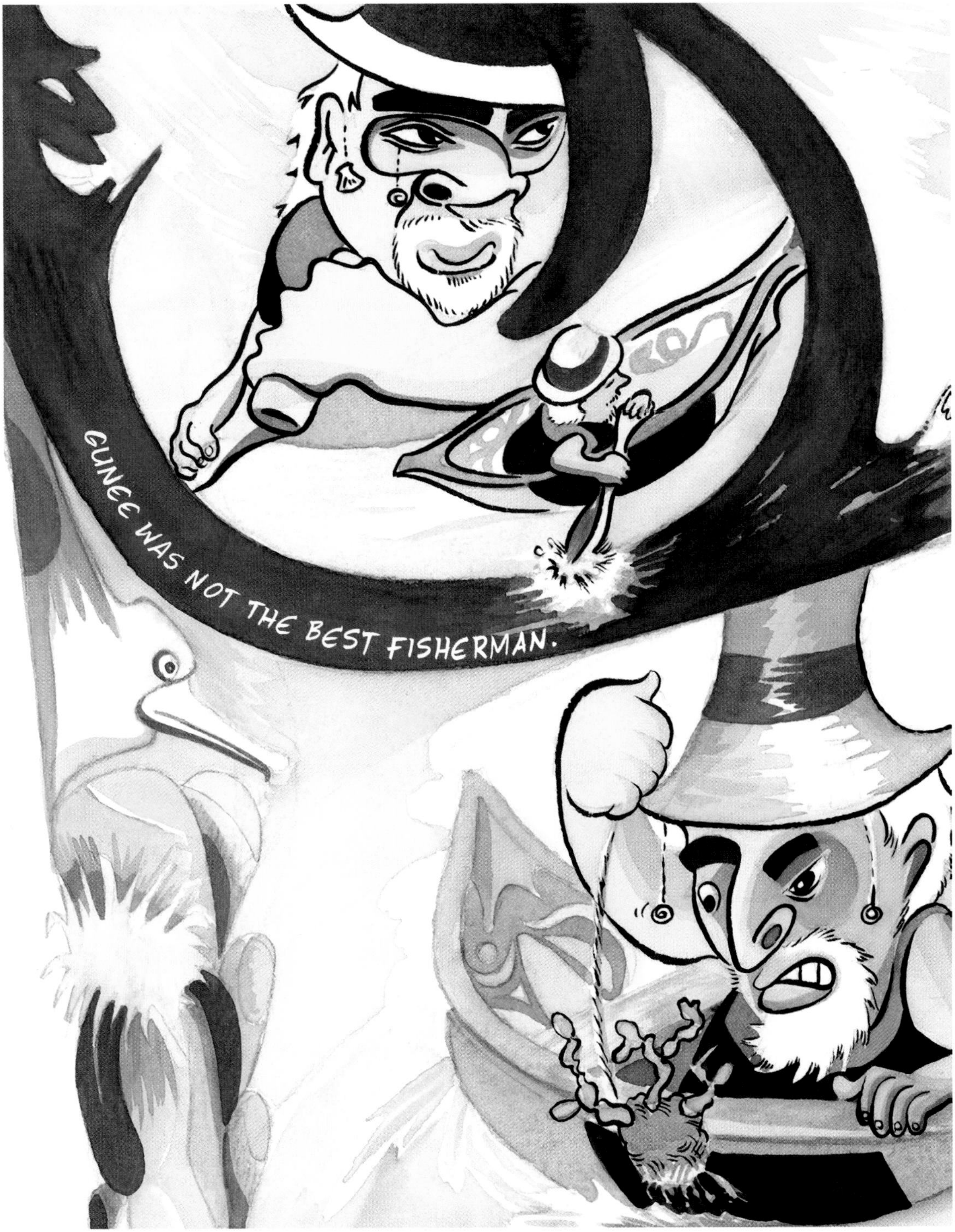
GUNEE WAS NOT THE BEST FISHERMAN.

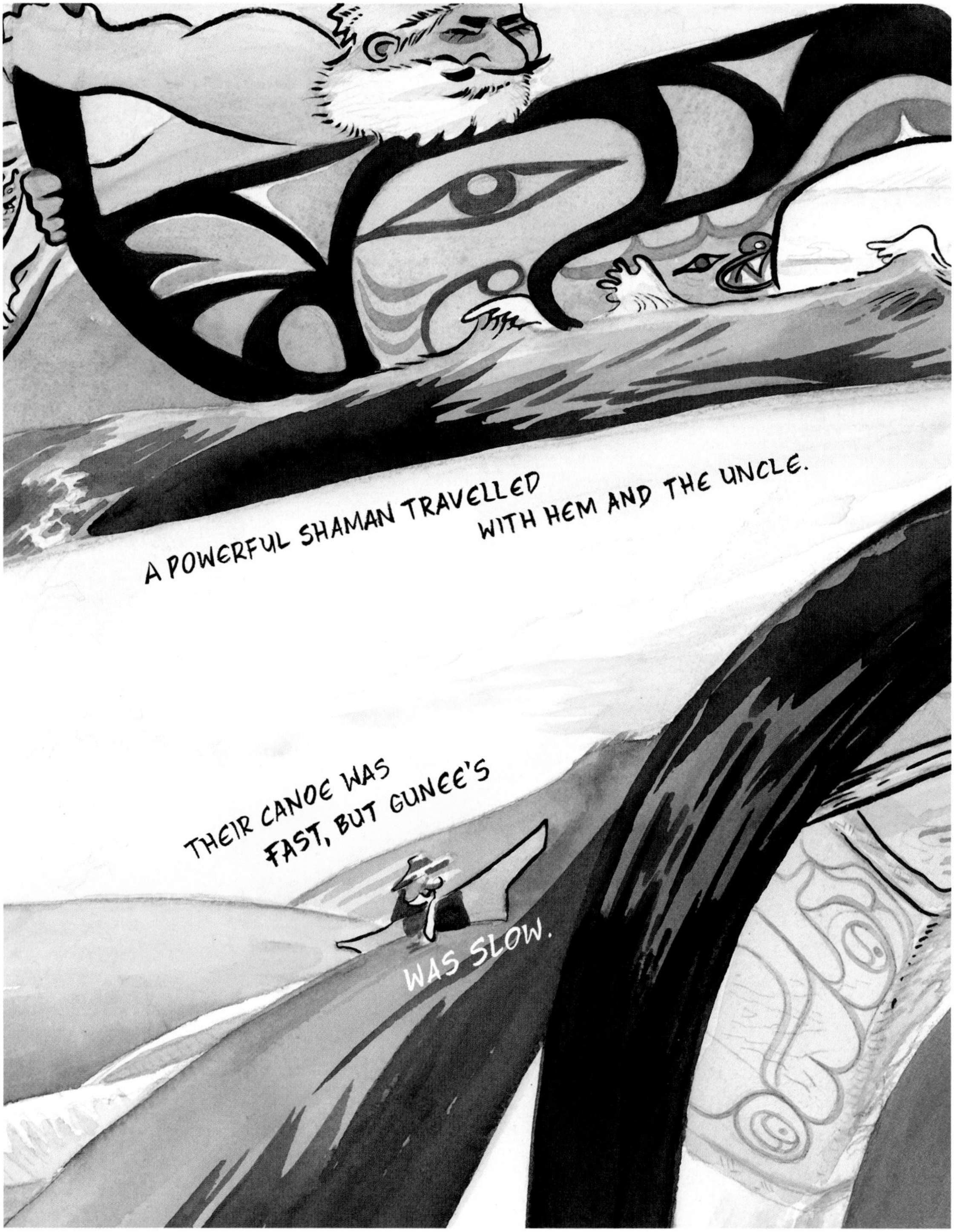
A POWERFUL SHAMAN TRAVELLED
WITH HEM AND THE UNCLE.
THEIR CANOE WAS
FAST, BUT GUNEE'S
WAS SLOW.

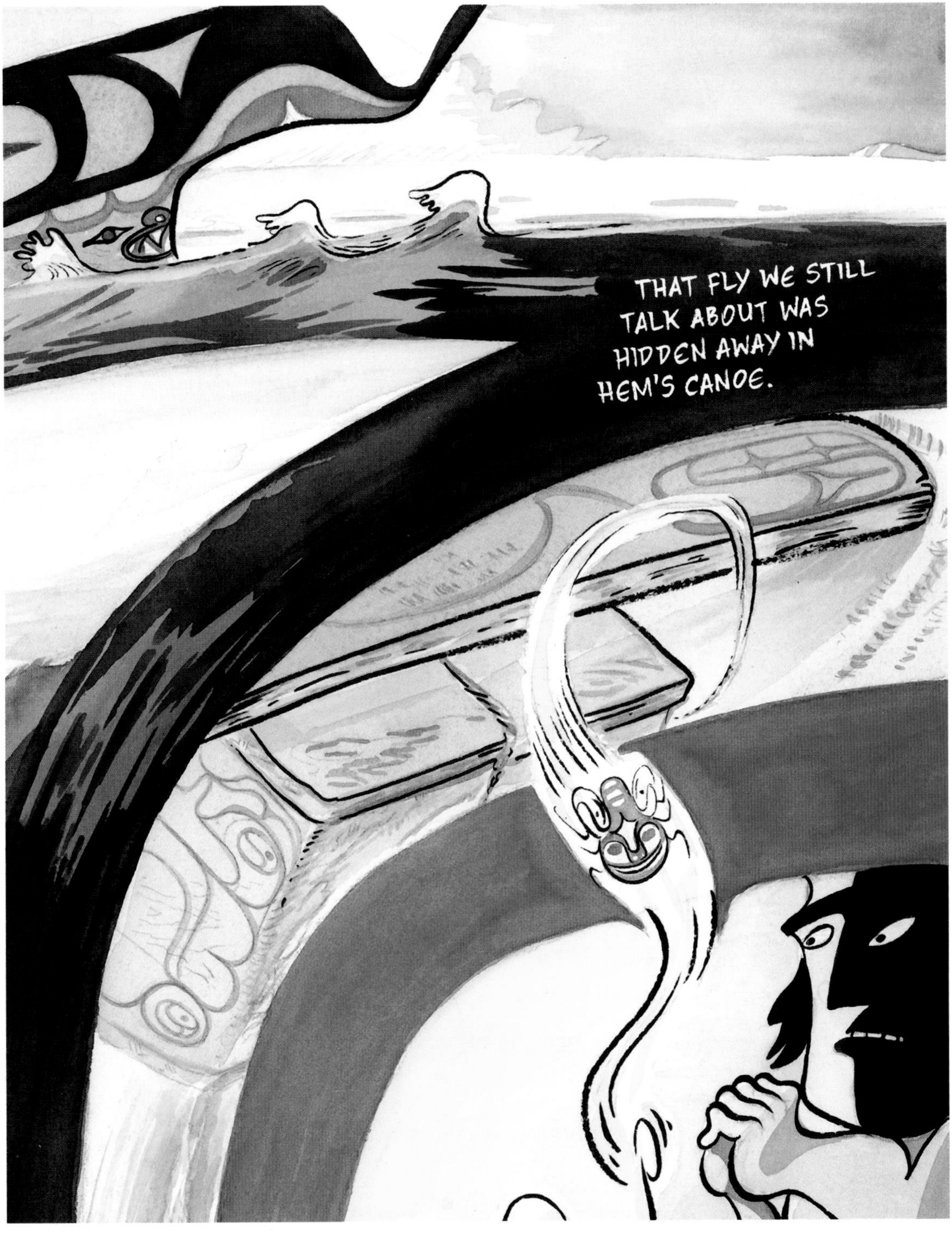
THAT FLY WE STILL TALK ABOUT WAS HIDDEN AWAY IN HEM'S CANOE.

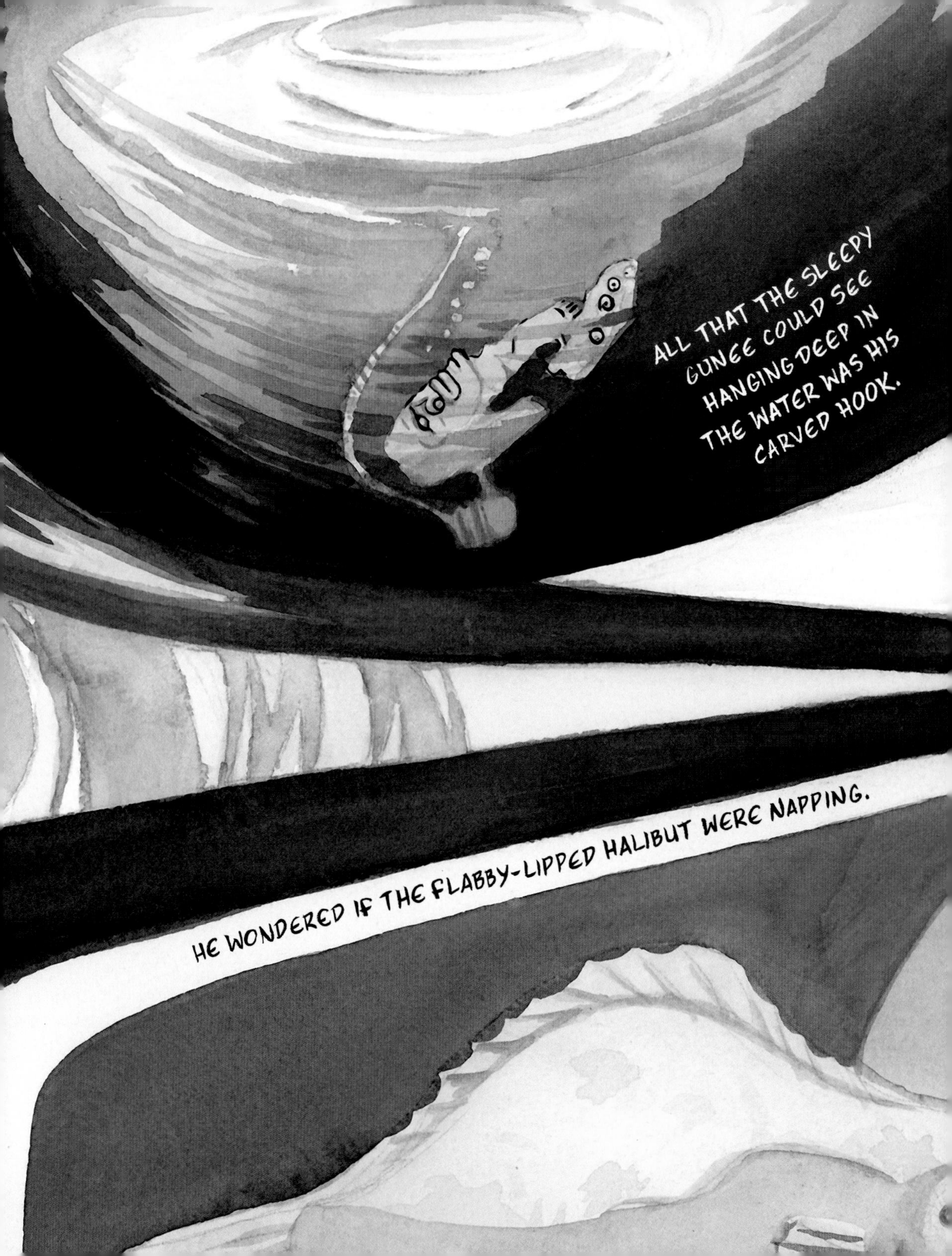
ALL THAT THE SLEEPY GUNEE COULD SEE HANGING DEEP IN THE WATER WAS HIS CARVED HOOK.
HE WONDERED IF THE FLABBY-LIPPED HALIBUT WERE NAPPING.

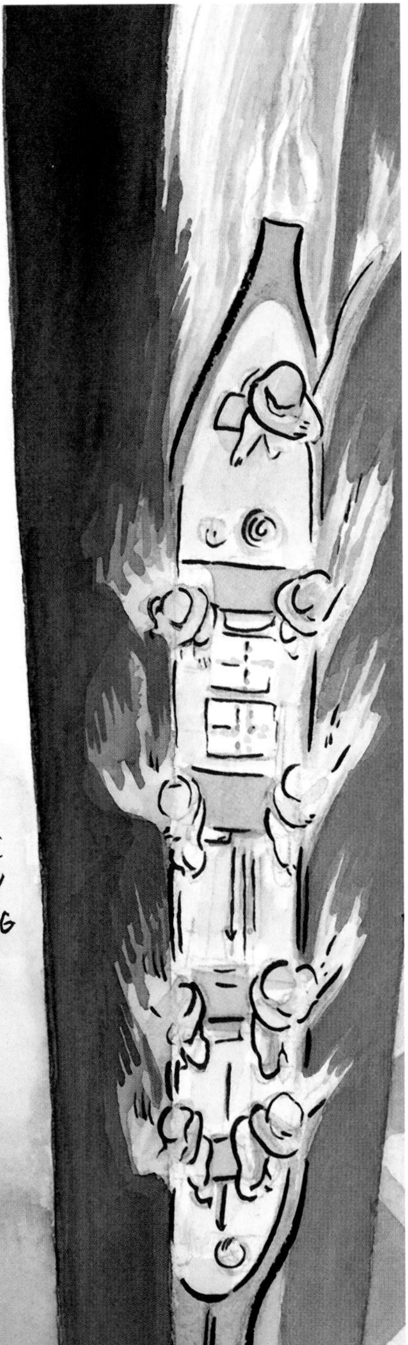

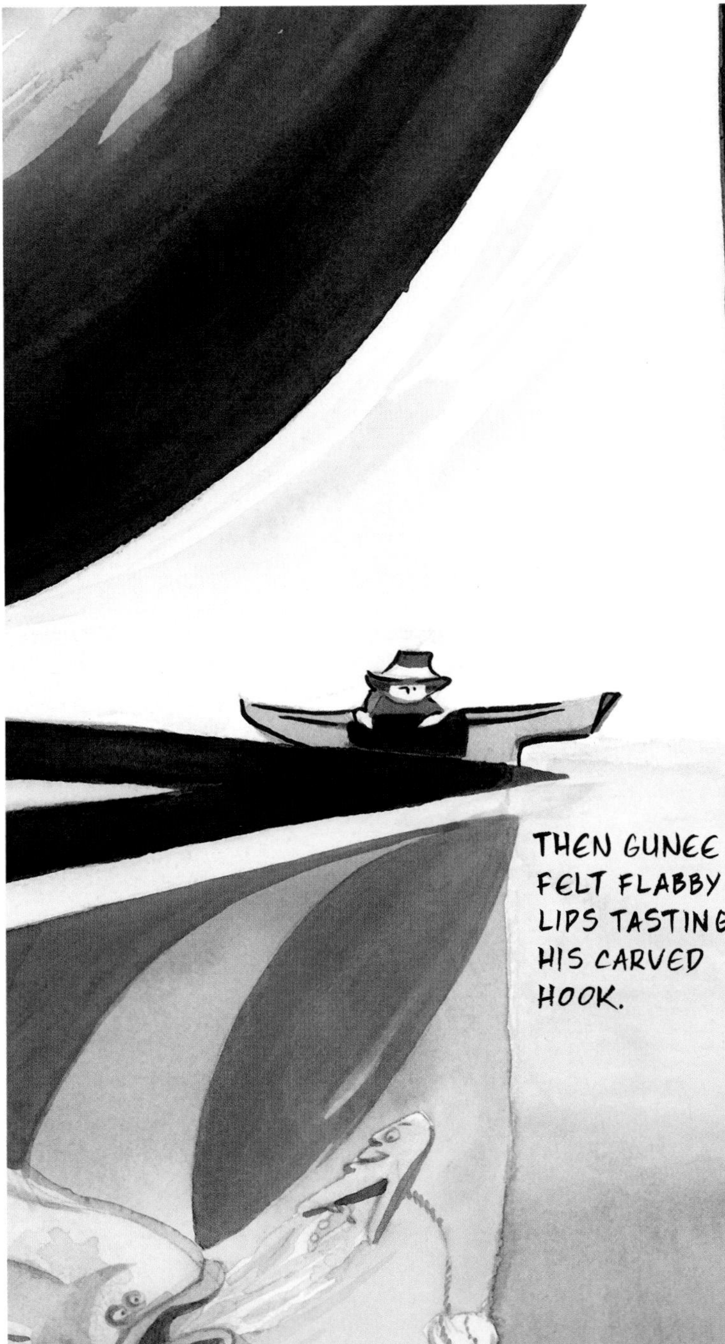
THEN GUNEE FELT FLABBY LIPS TASTING HIS CARVED HOOK.

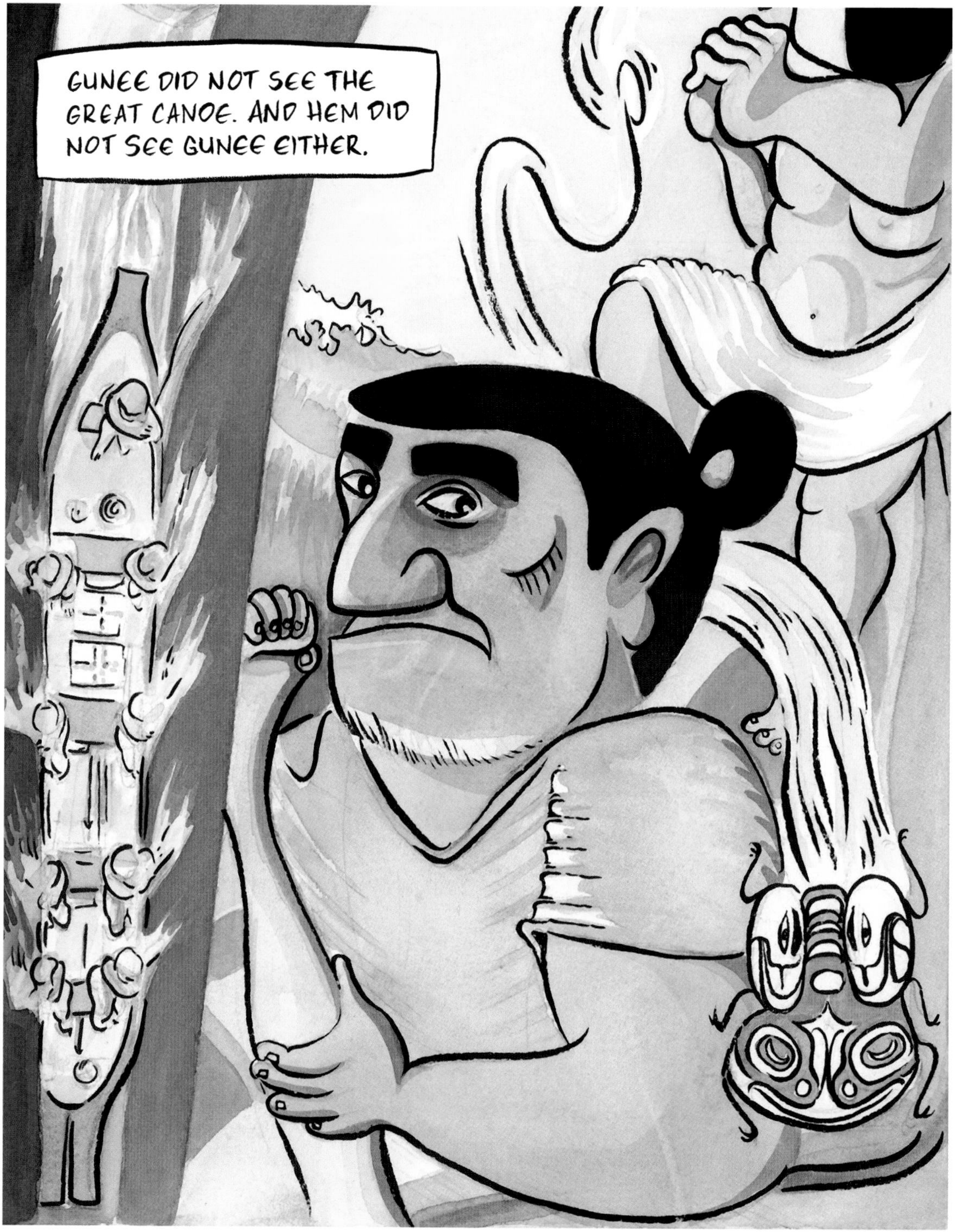
GUNEE DID NOT SEE THE GREAT CANOE. AND HEM DID NOT SEE GUNEE EITHER.

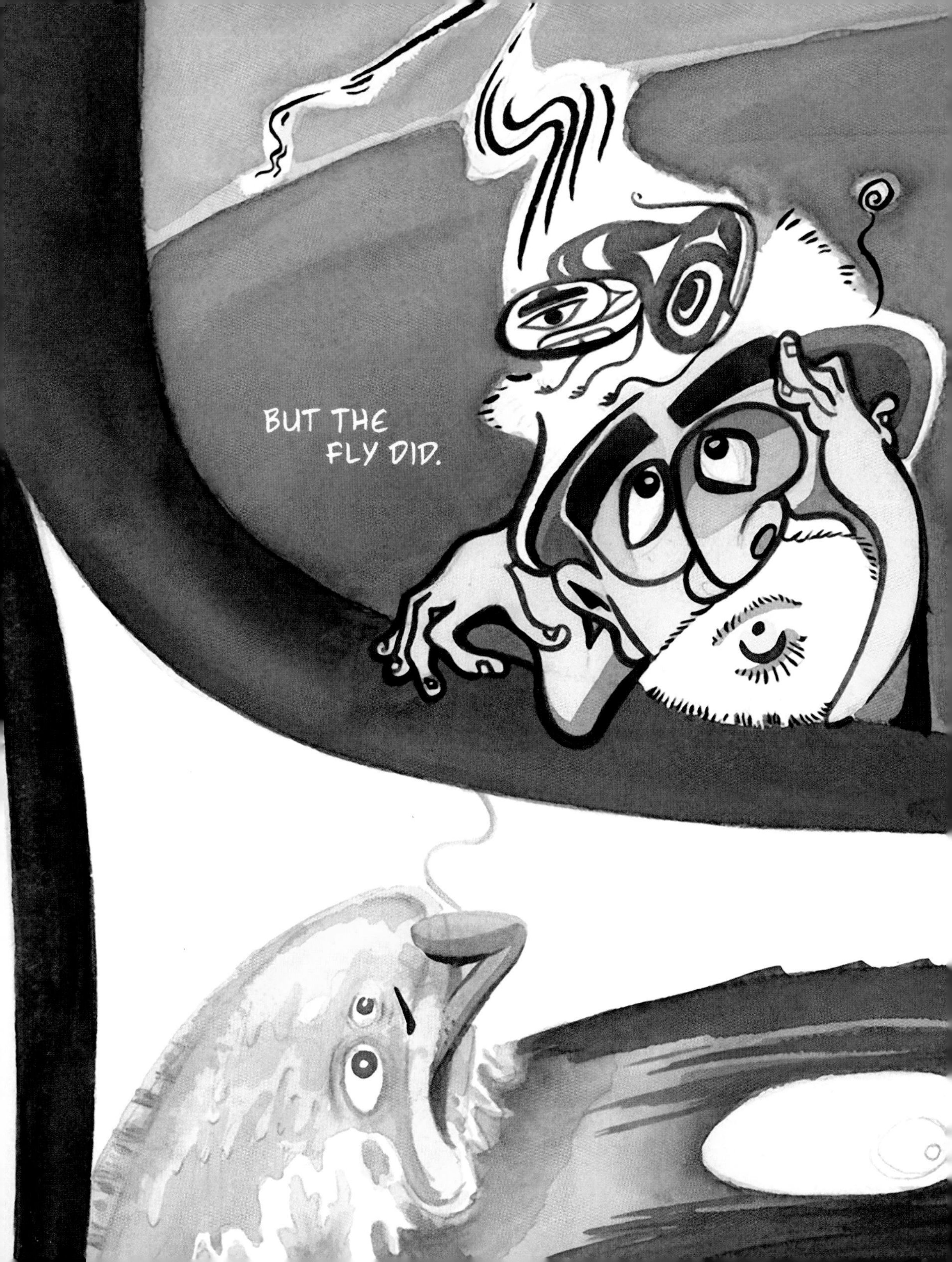
BUT THE FLY DID.

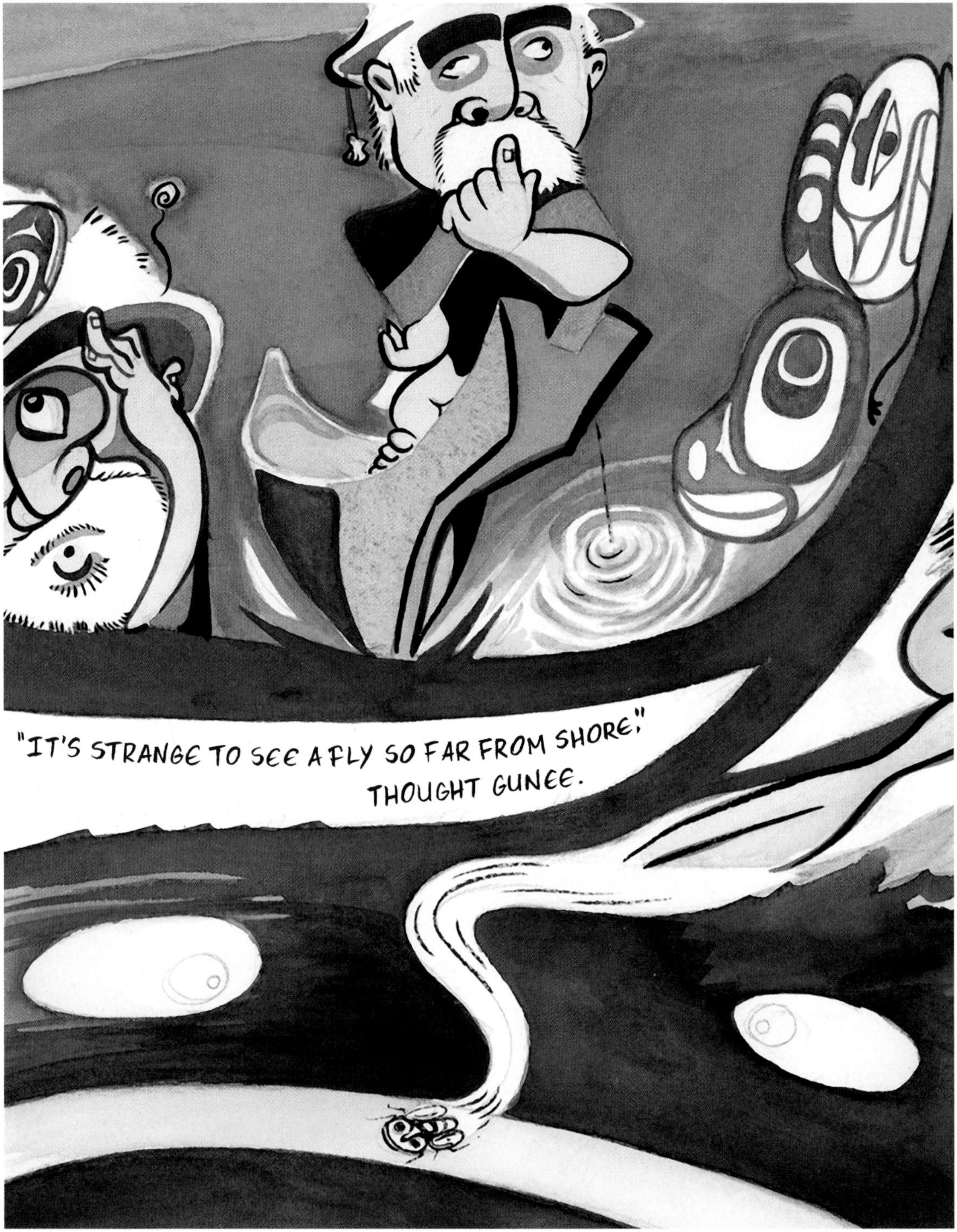
"IT'S STRANGE TO SEE A FLY SO FAR FROM SHORE,"
THOUGHT GUNEE.

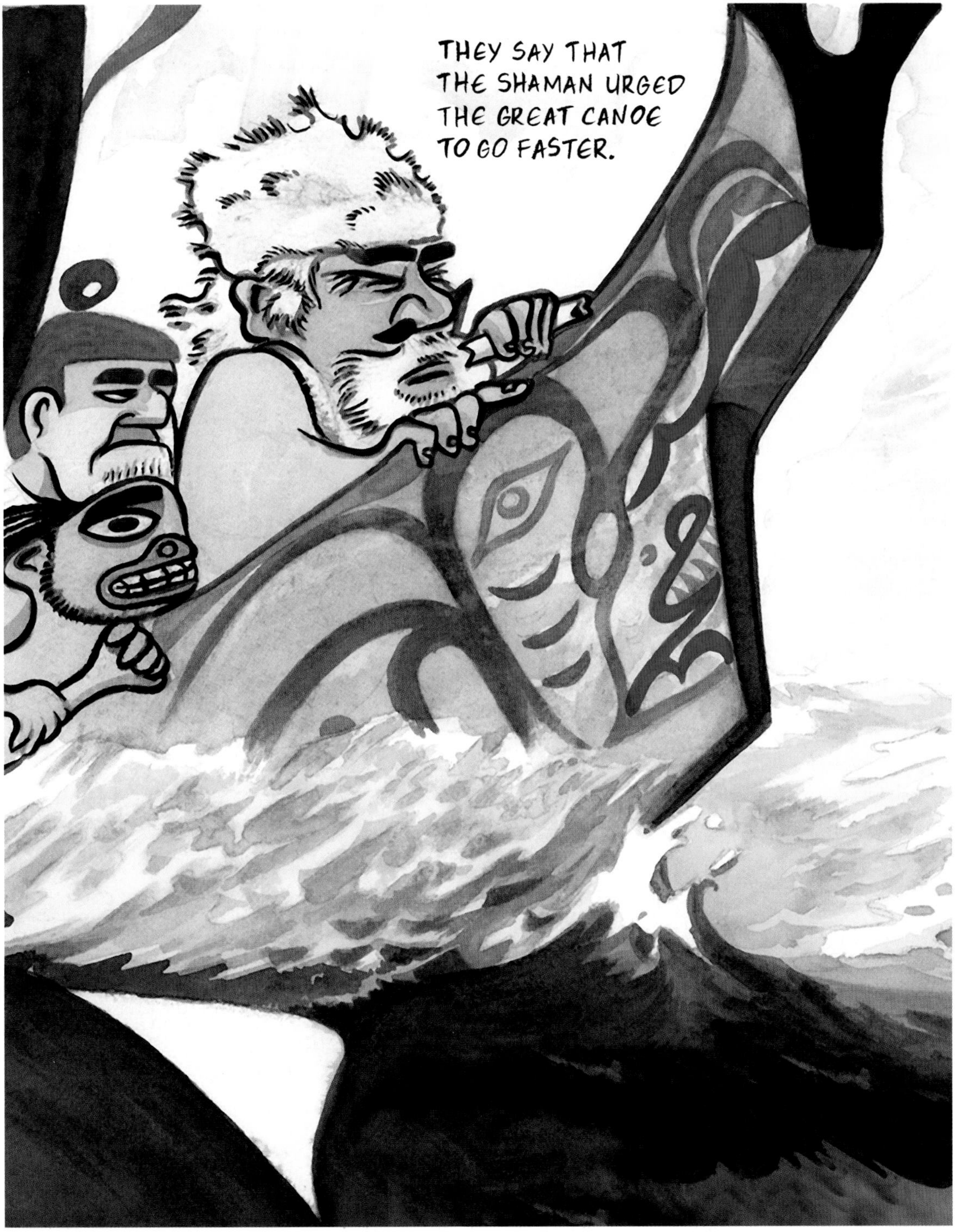
THEY SAY THAT THE SHAMAN URGED THE GREAT CANOE TO GO FASTER.

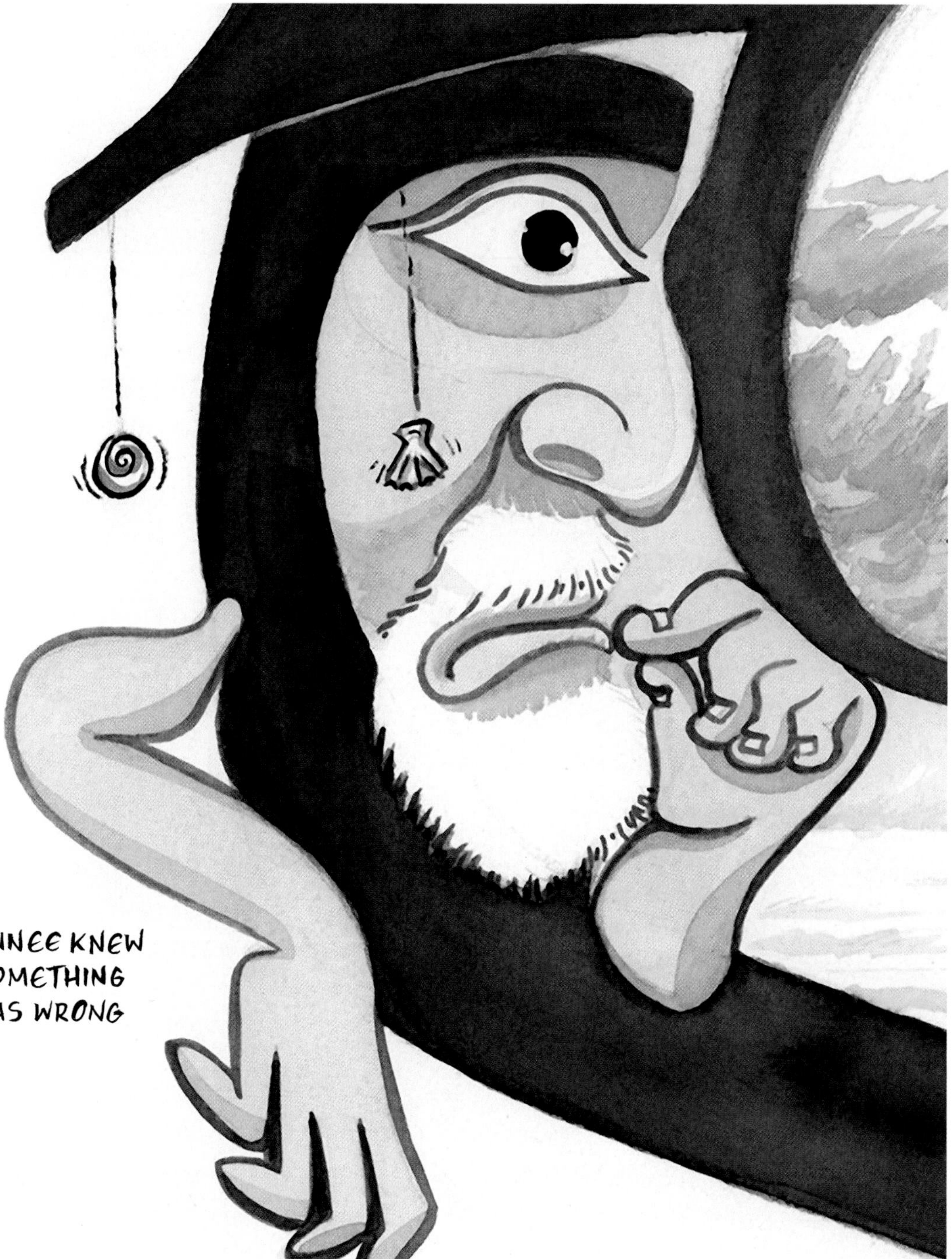

GUNEE KNEW
SOMETHING
WAS WRONG

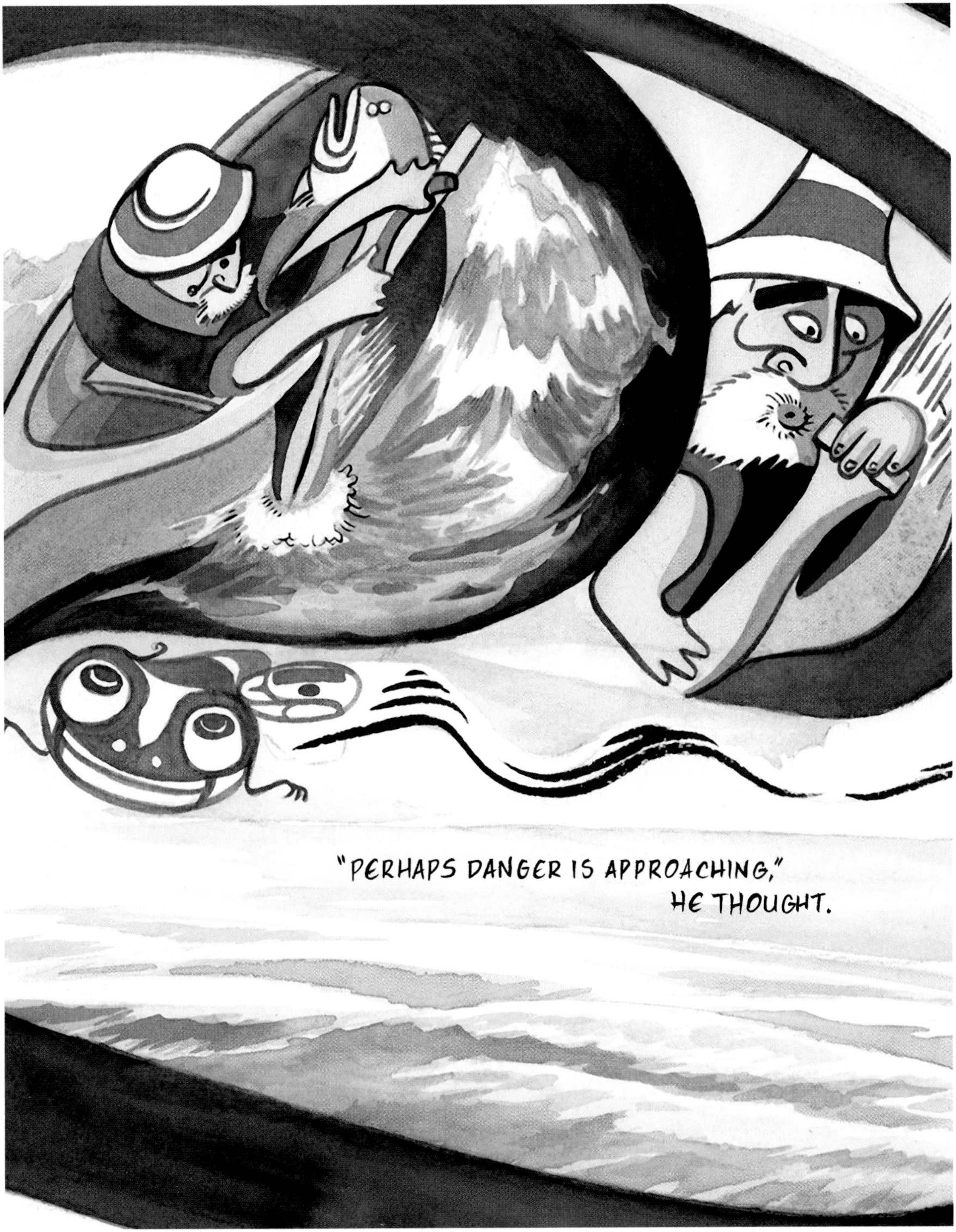
"PERHAPS DANGER IS APPROACHING,"
HE THOUGHT.

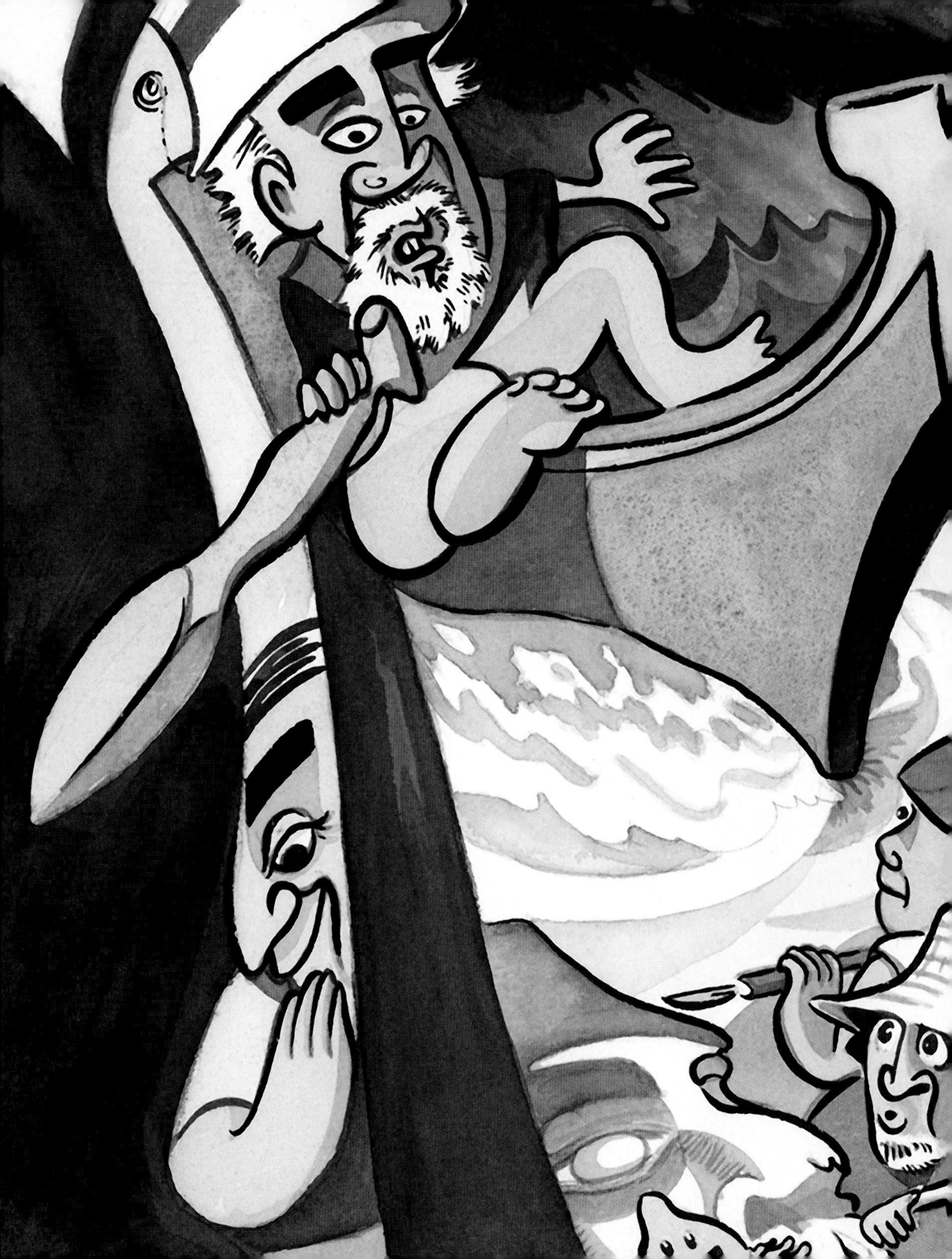

SO HE RACED HIS CANOE
BACK TO THE TOWN AND
WARNED EVERYONE.

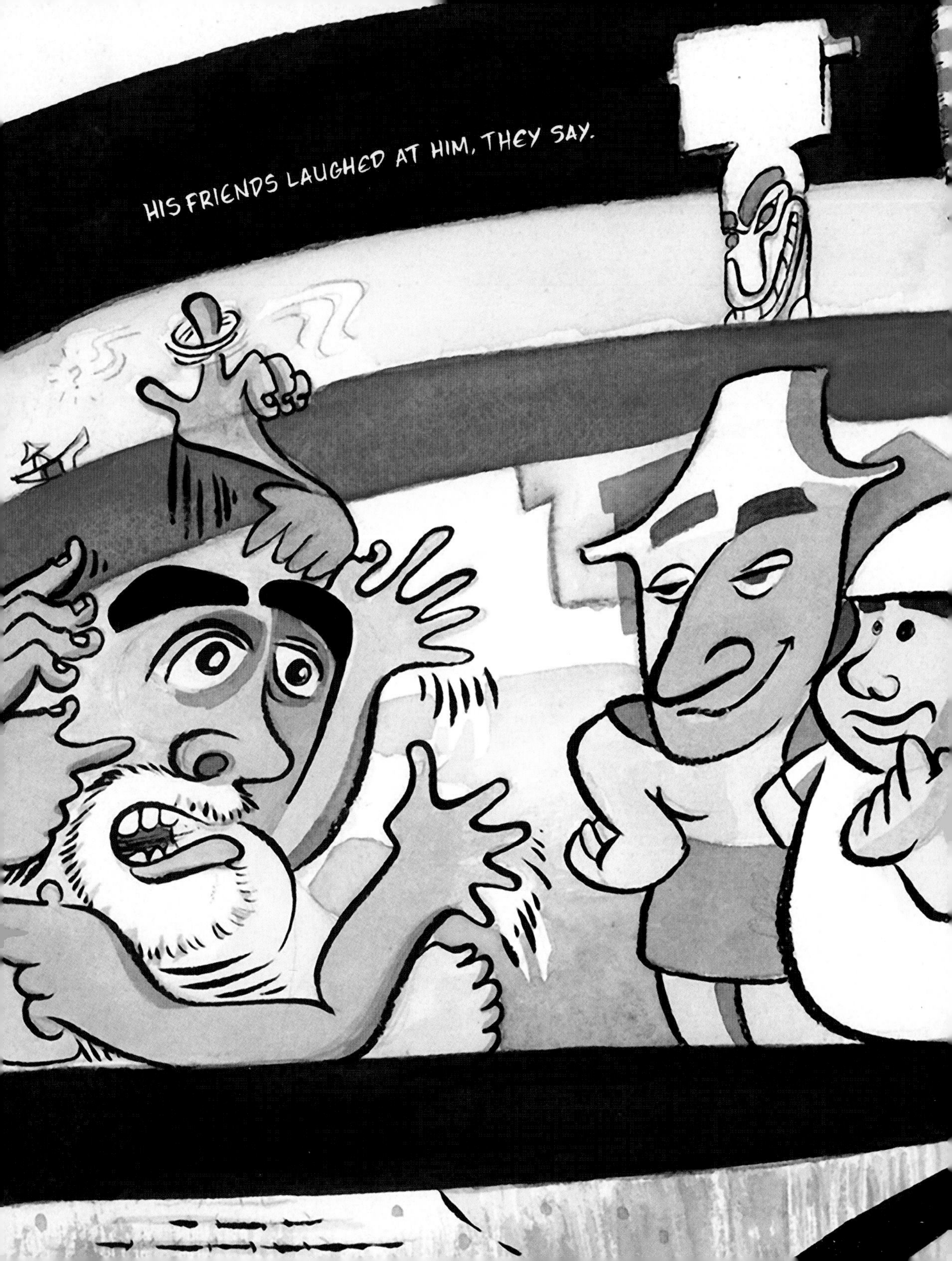
HIS FRIENDS LAUGHED AT HIM, THEY SAY.

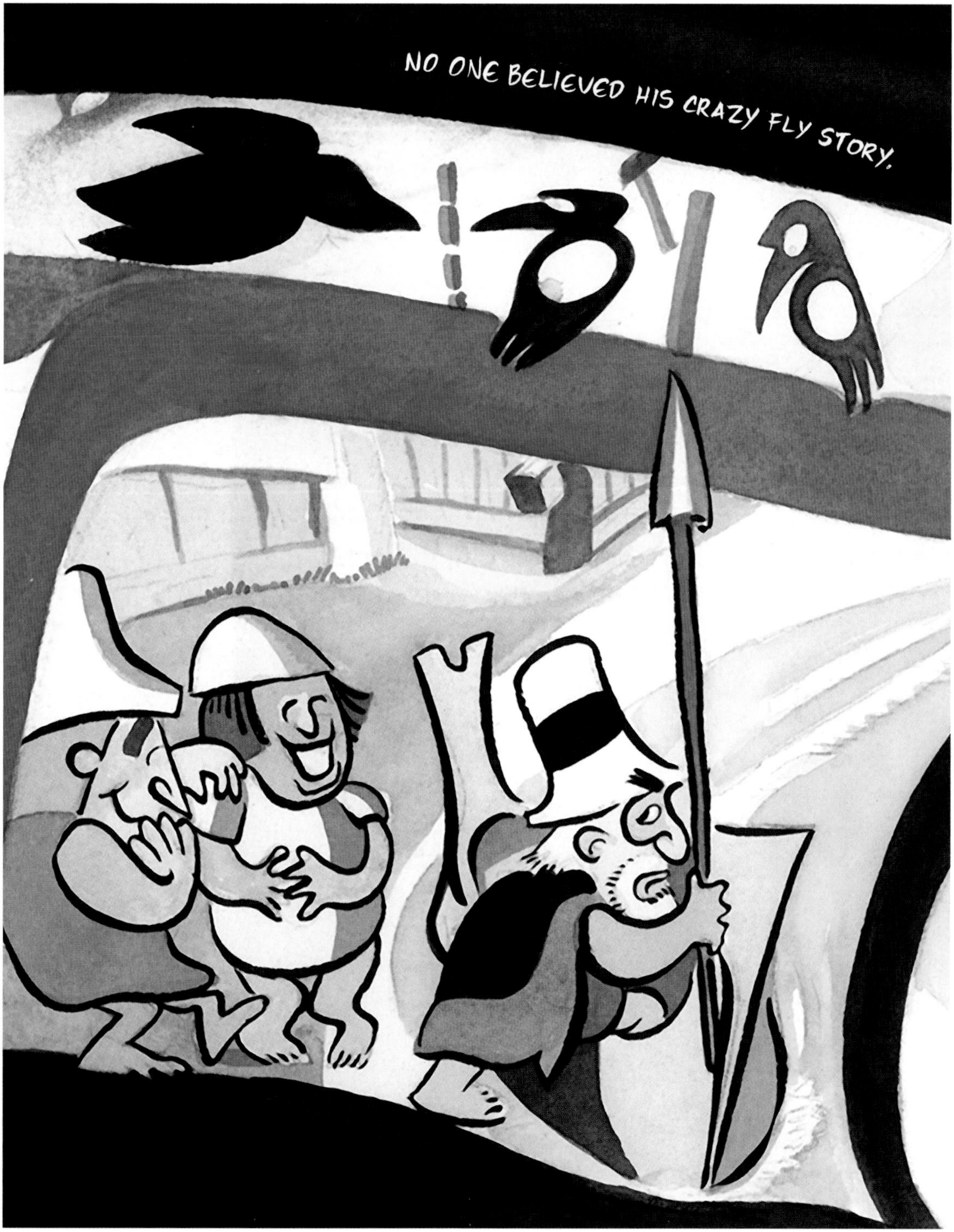
NO ONE BELIEVED HIS CRAZY FLY STORY.

BUT AFTER GUNEE LEFT THE
BEACH A STRANGE FLY WAS SEEN
IN THE VILLAGE.

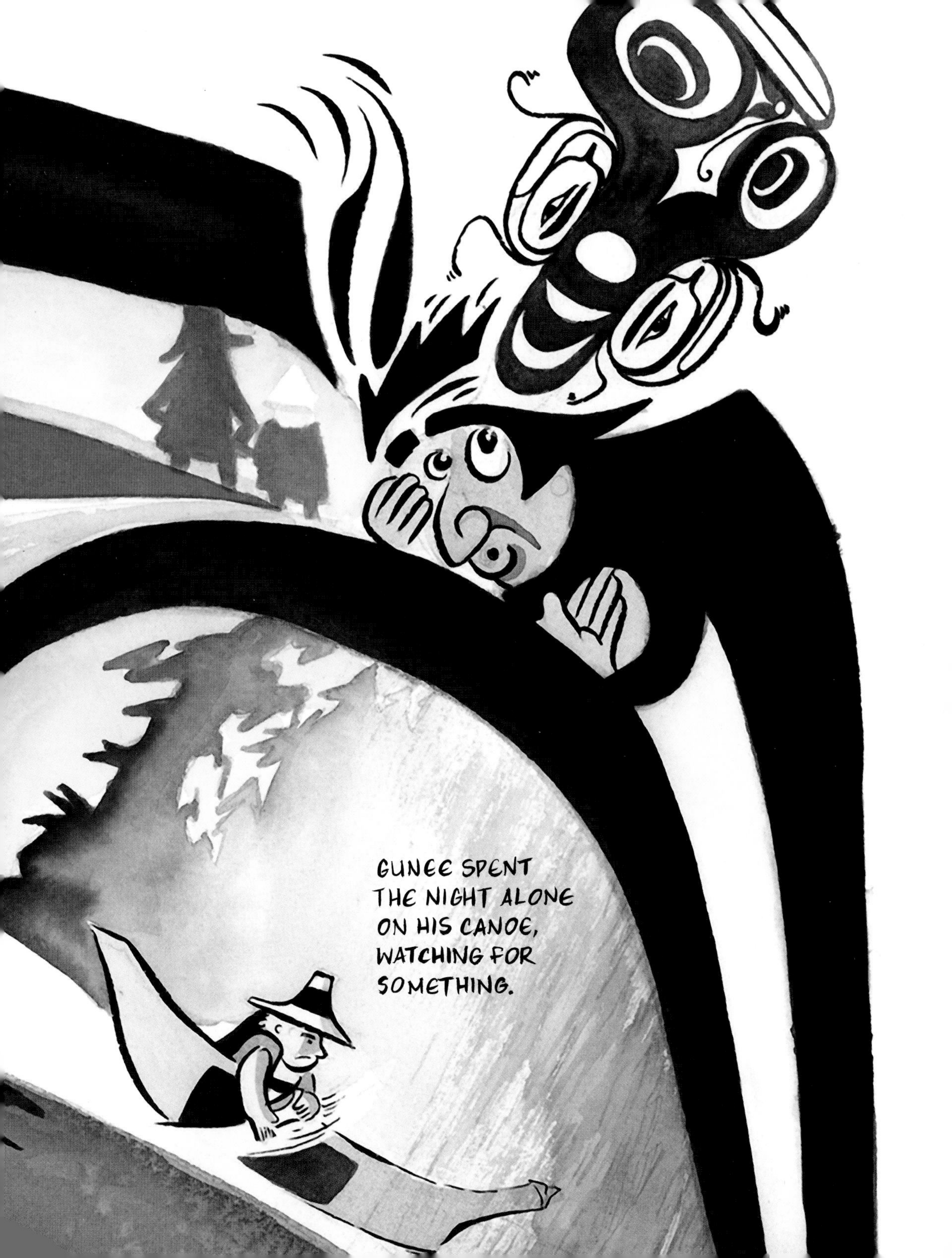
GUNEE SPENT THE NIGHT ALONE ON HIS CANOE, WATCHING FOR SOMETHING.

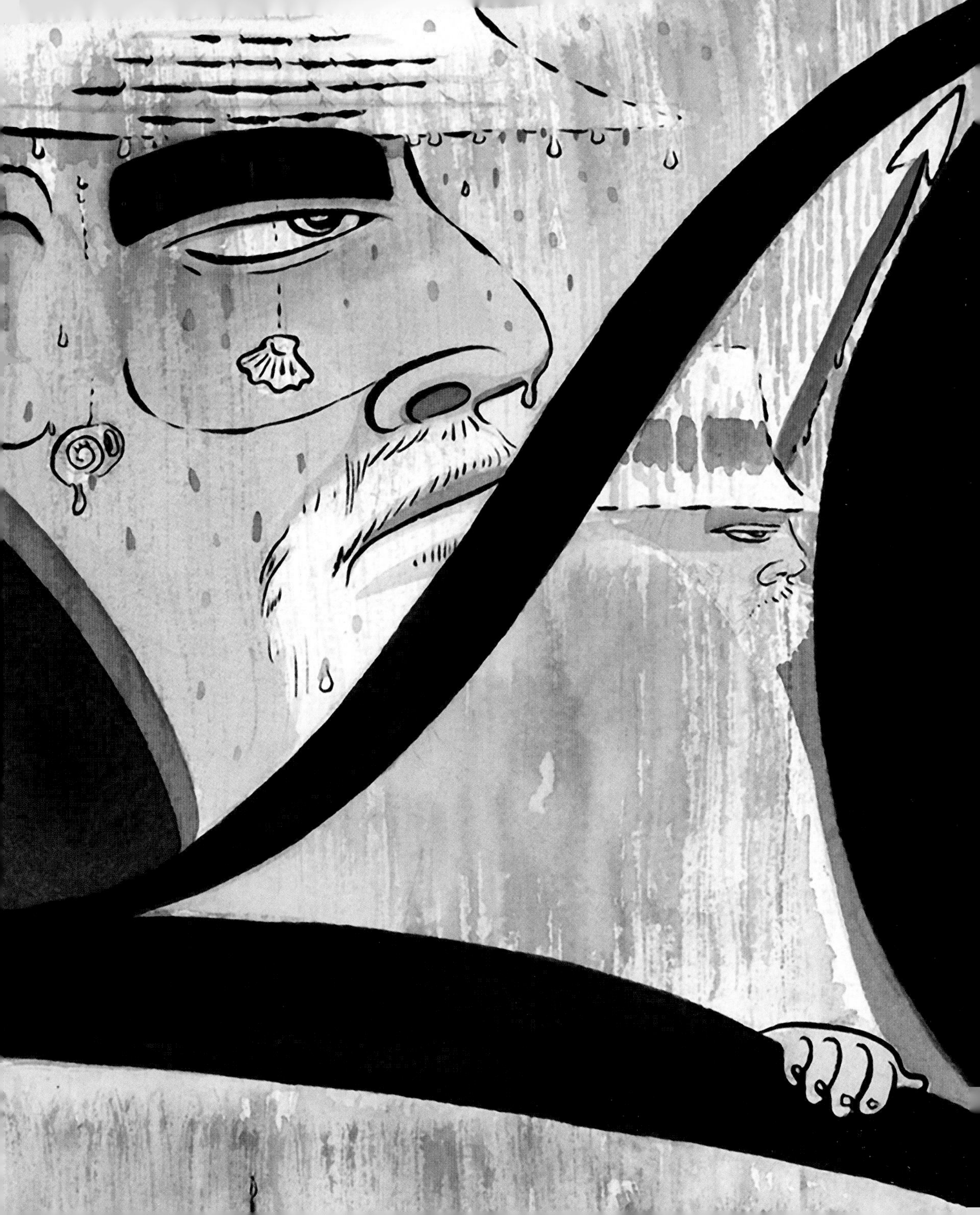

AND EVEN AS HEM'S UNSEEN CANOE
CAME CLOSER TO THE ISLANDS,
GUNEE'S FRIENDS BEGAN TO WORRY.

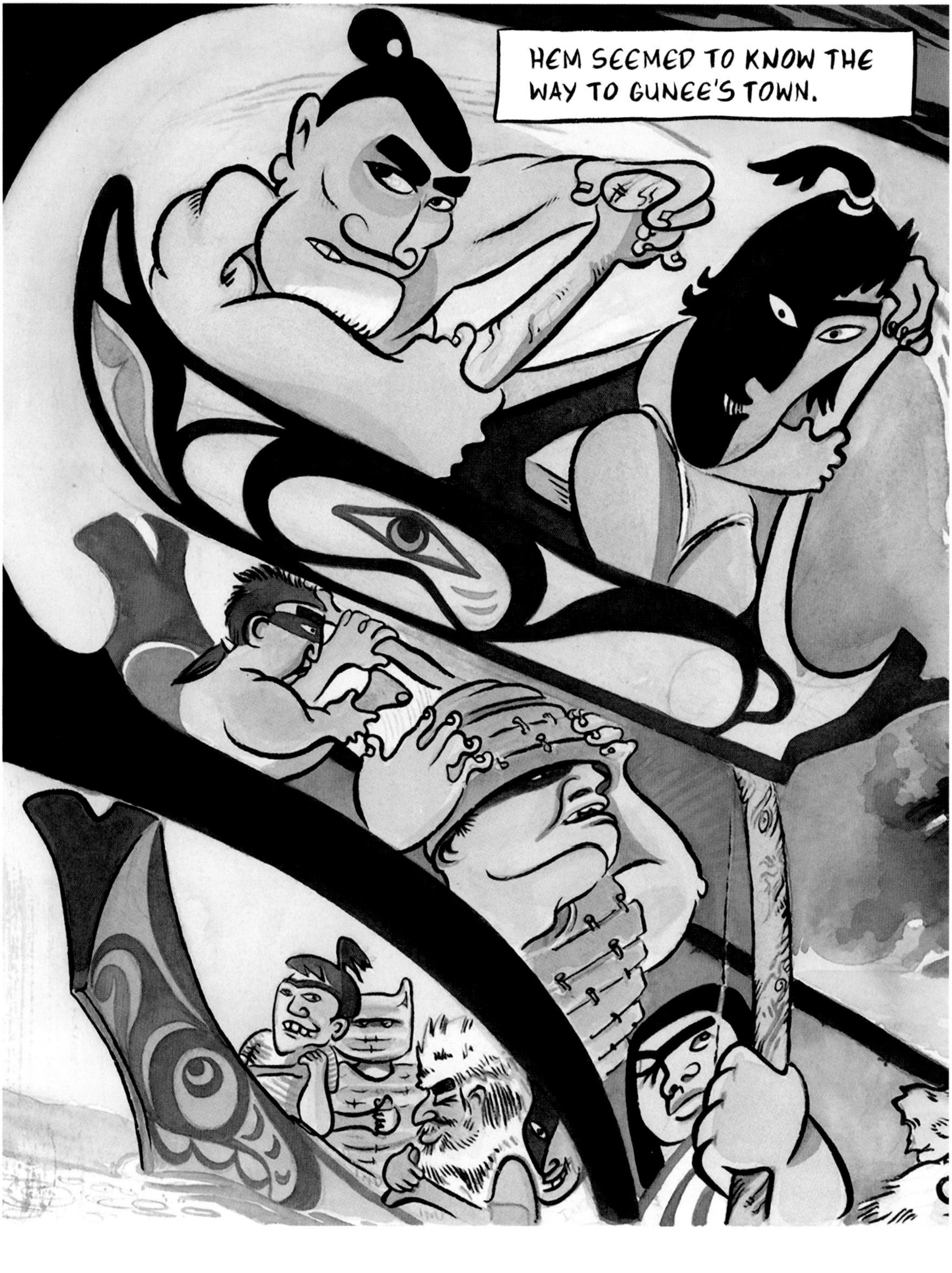
HEM SEEMED TO KNOW THE WAY TO GUNEE'S TOWN.

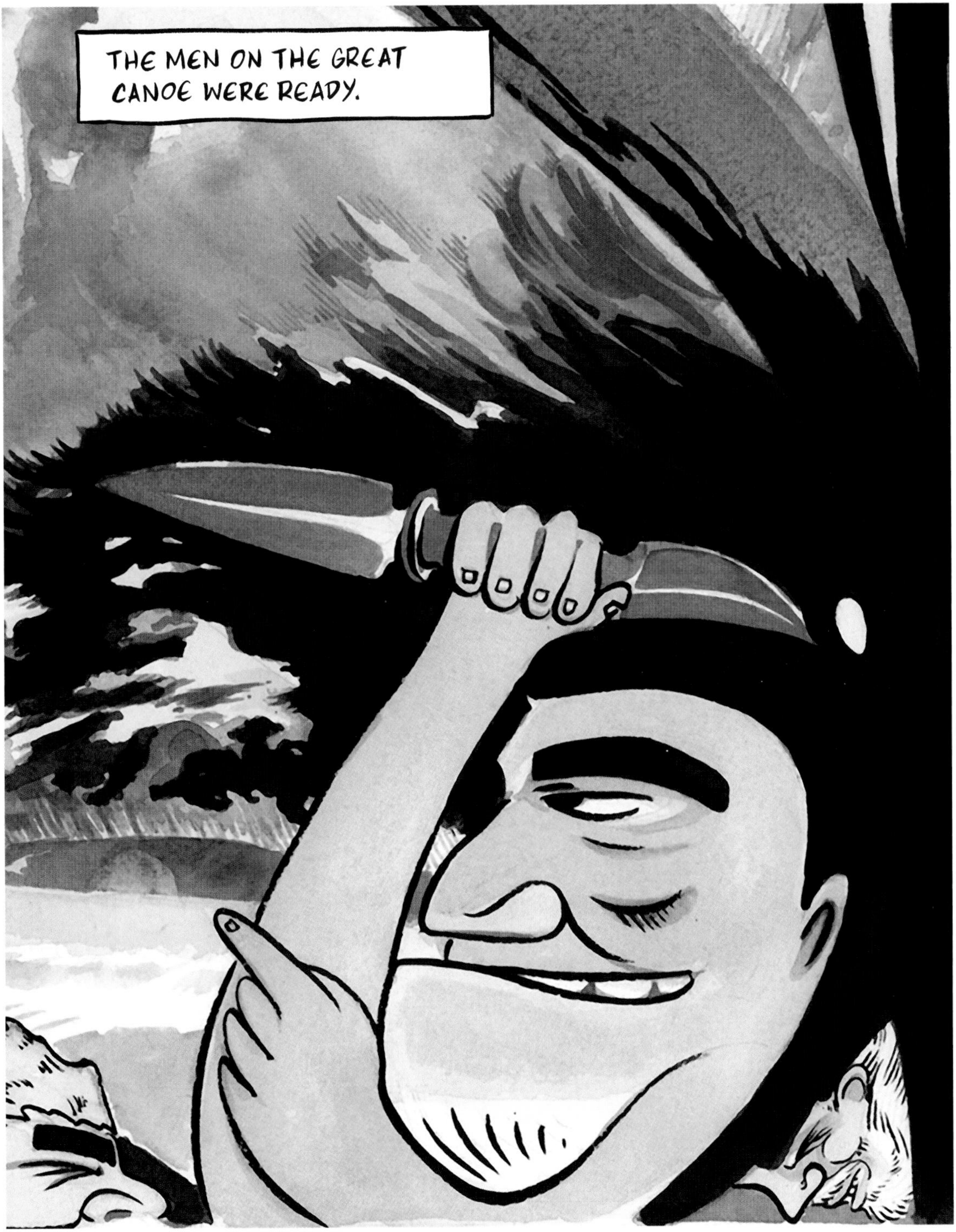
THE MEN ON THE GREAT CANOE WERE READY.

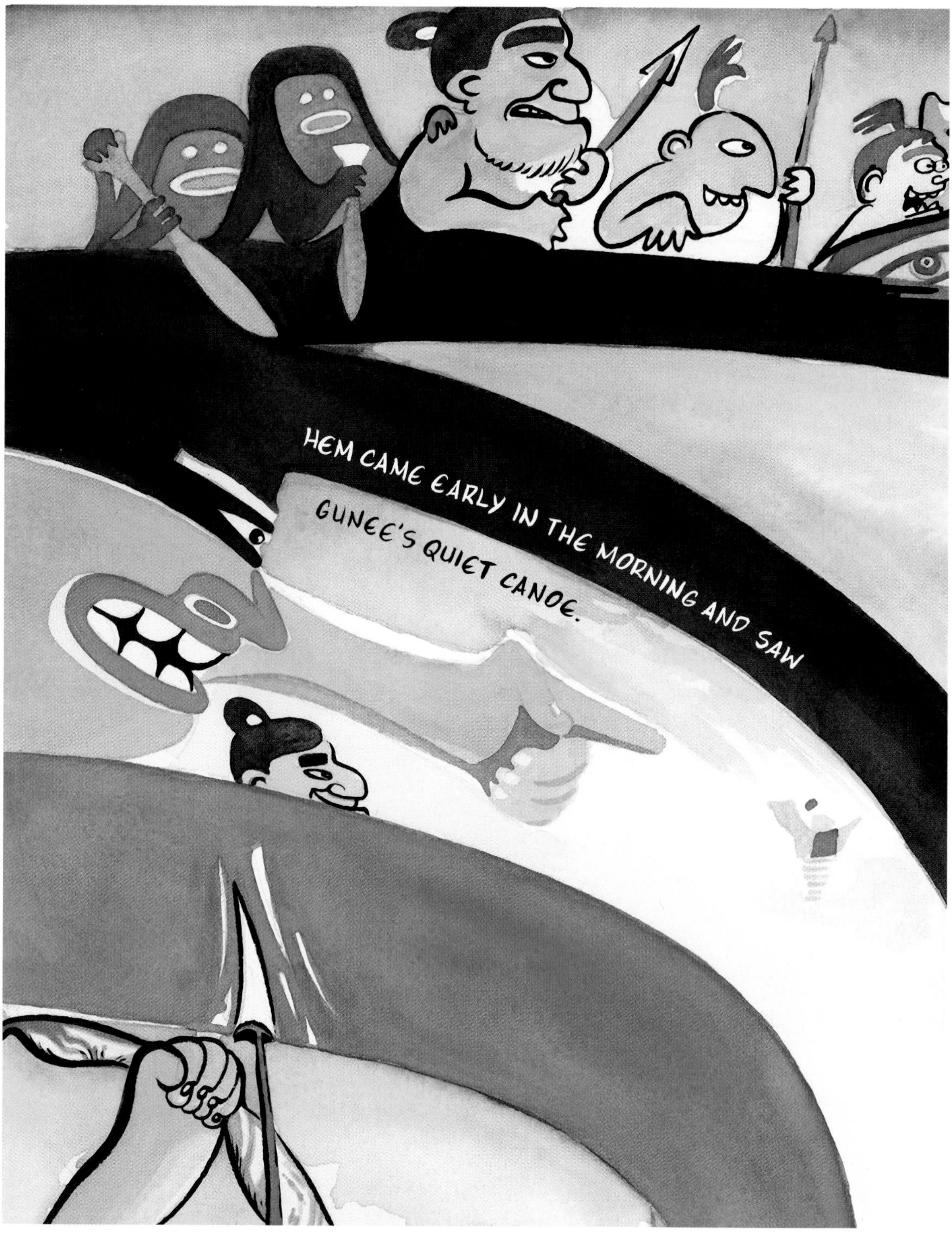
HEM CAME EARLY IN THE MORNING AND SAW
GUNEE'S QUIET CANOE.

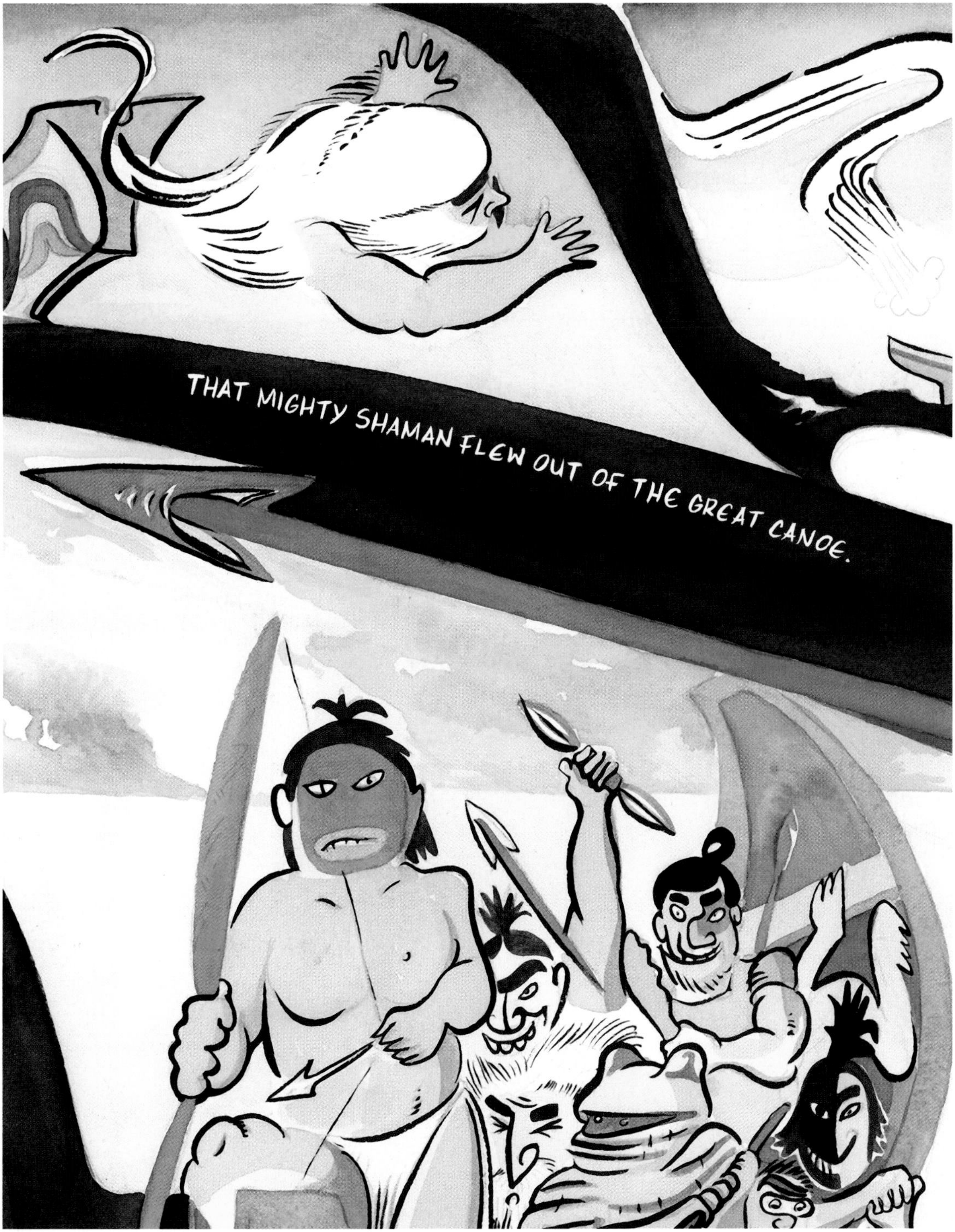
THAT MIGHTY SHAMAN FLEW OUT OF THE GREAT CANOE.

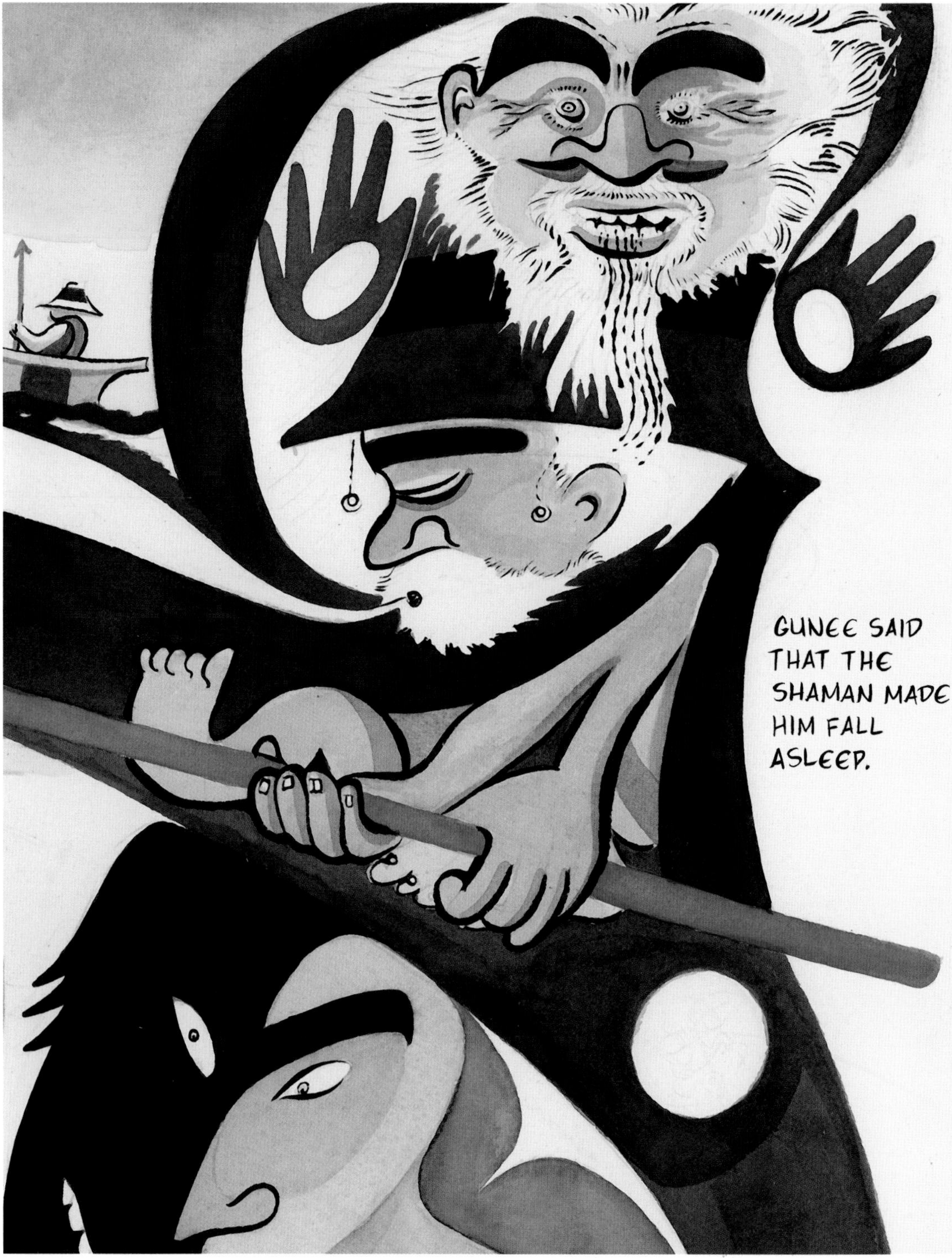
GUNEE SAID THAT THE SHAMAN MADE HIM FALL ASLEEP.

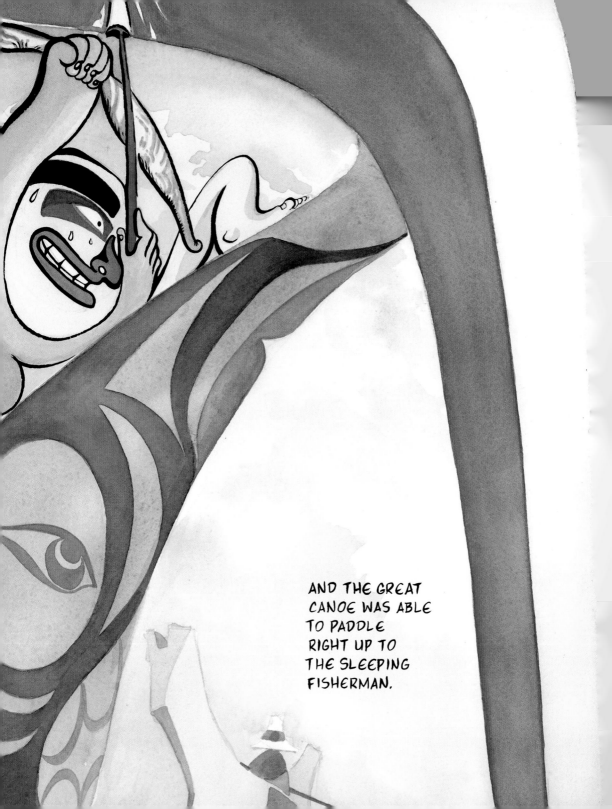

AND THE GREAT
CANOE WAS ABLE
TO PADDLE
RIGHT UP TO
THE SLEEPING
FISHERMAN.

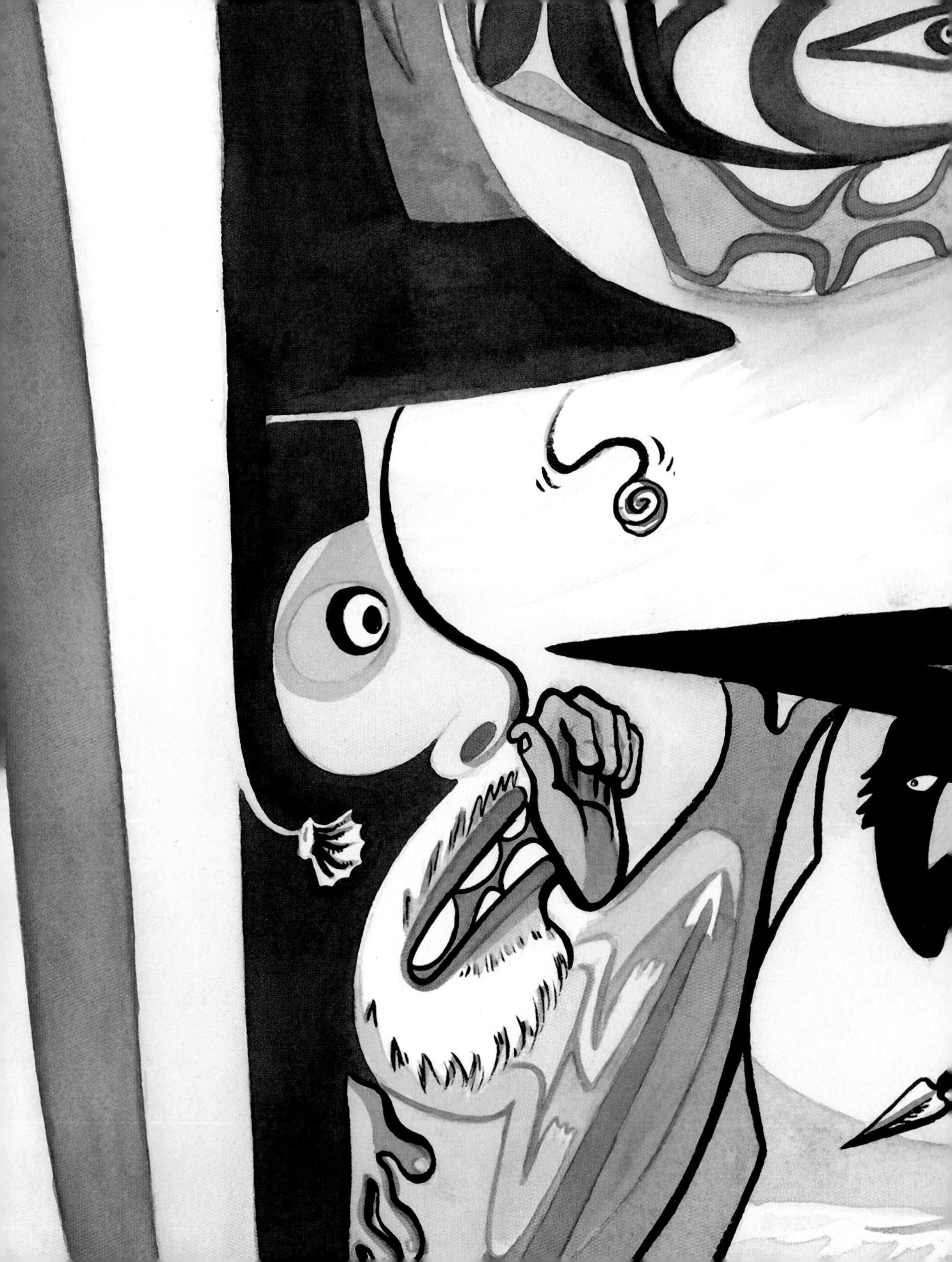

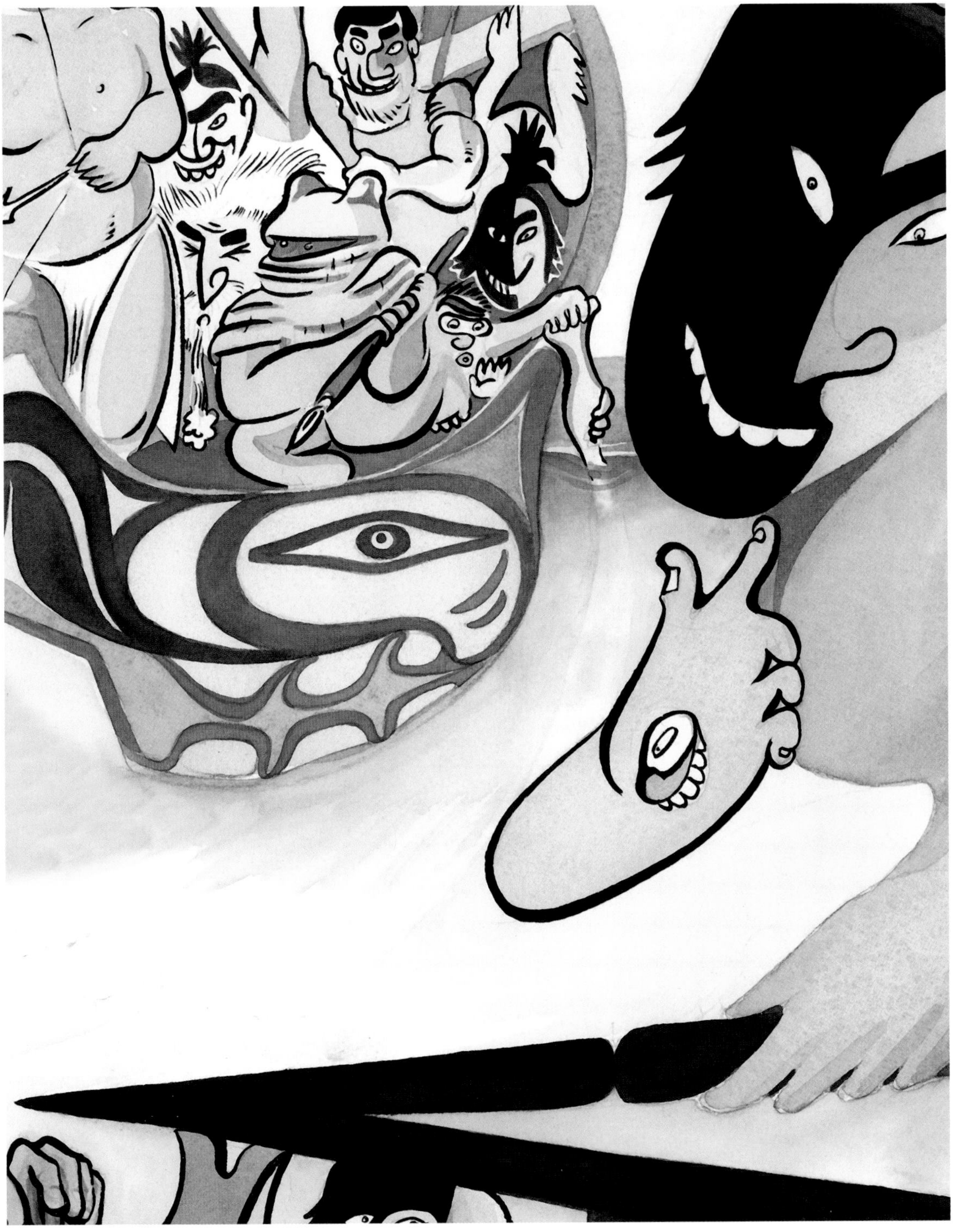

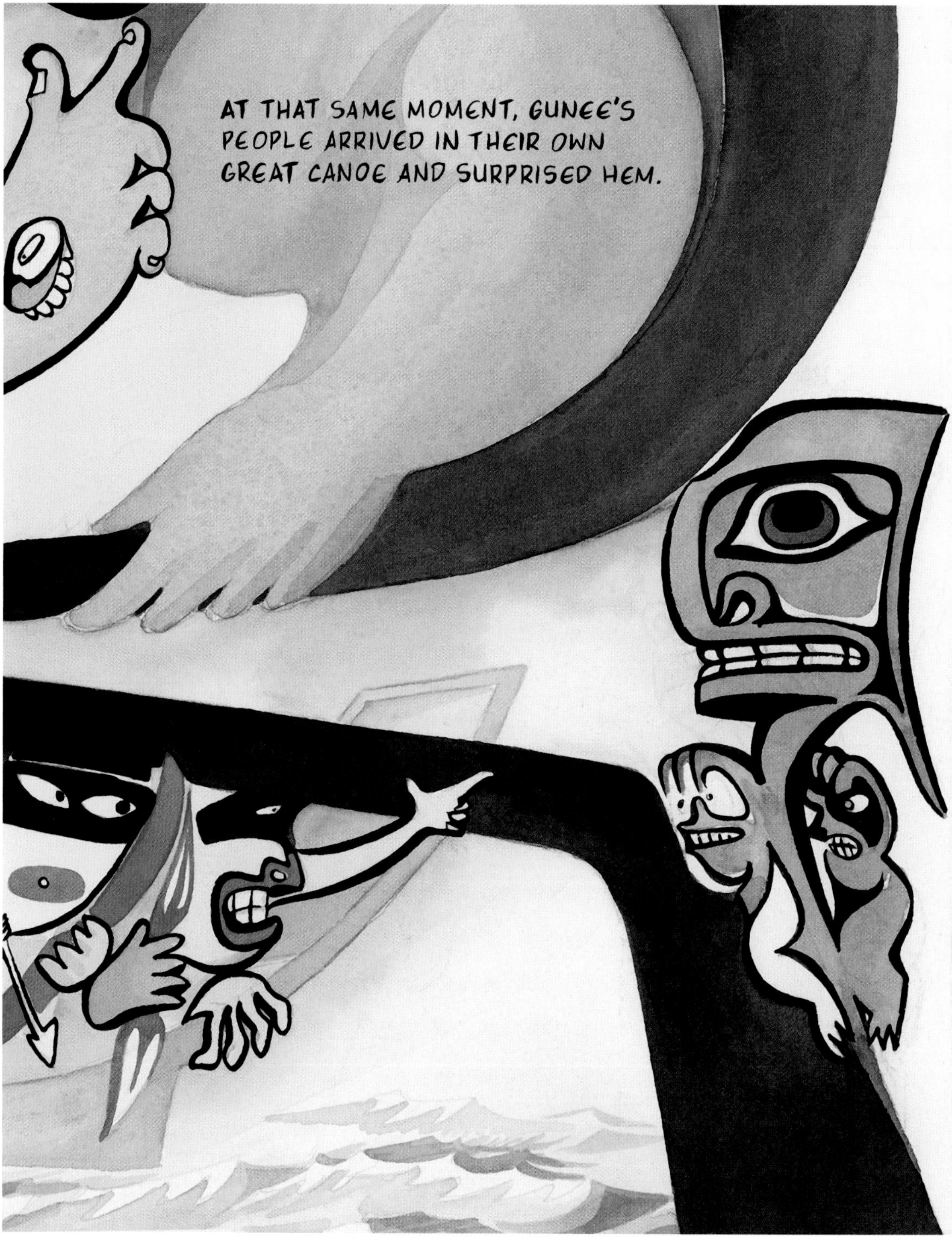
AT THAT SAME MOMENT, GUNEE'S PEOPLE ARRIVED IN THEIR OWN GREAT CANOE AND SURPRISED HEM.

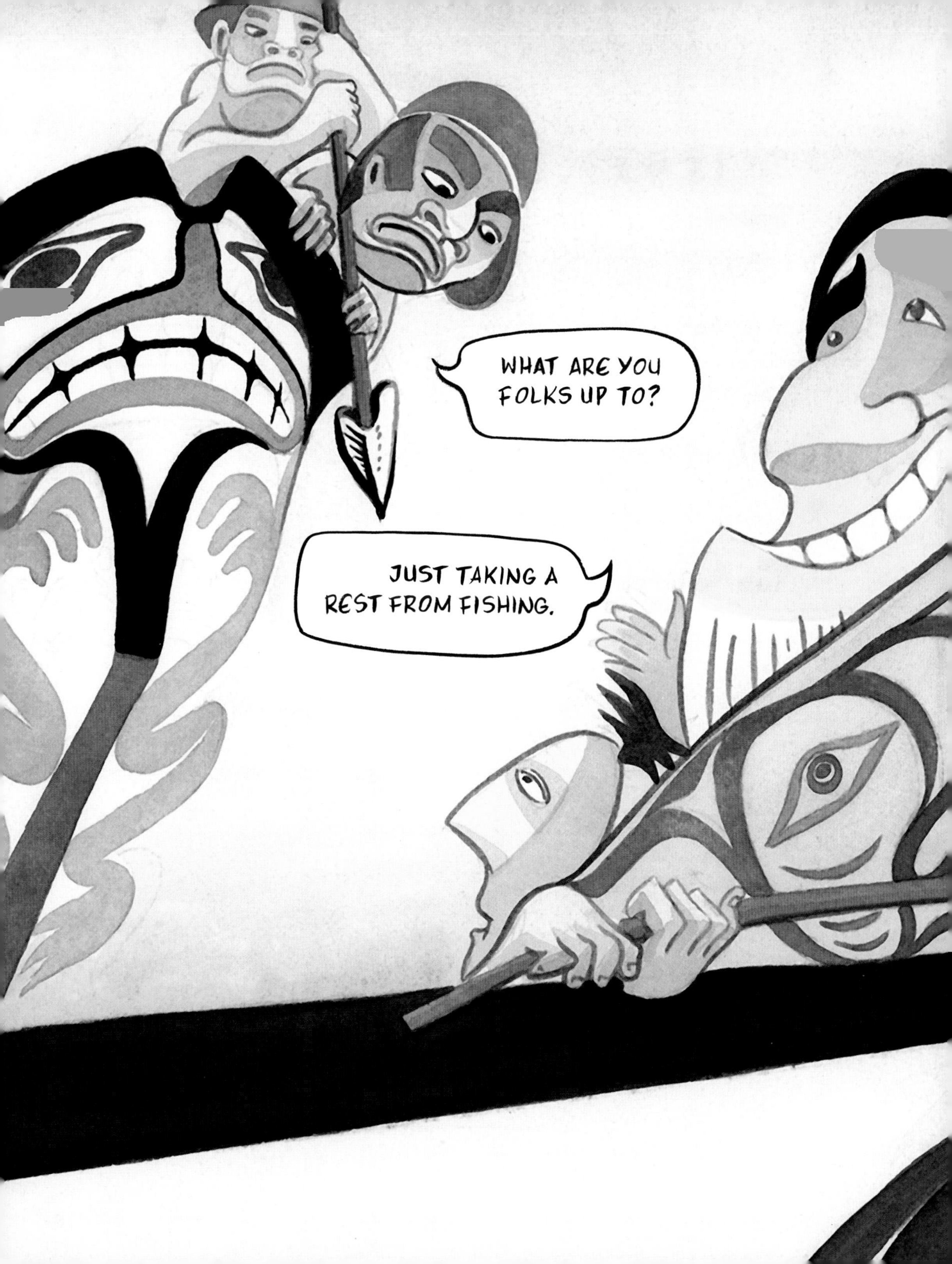
WHAT ARE YOU FOLKS UP TO?
JUST TAKING A REST FROM FISHING.

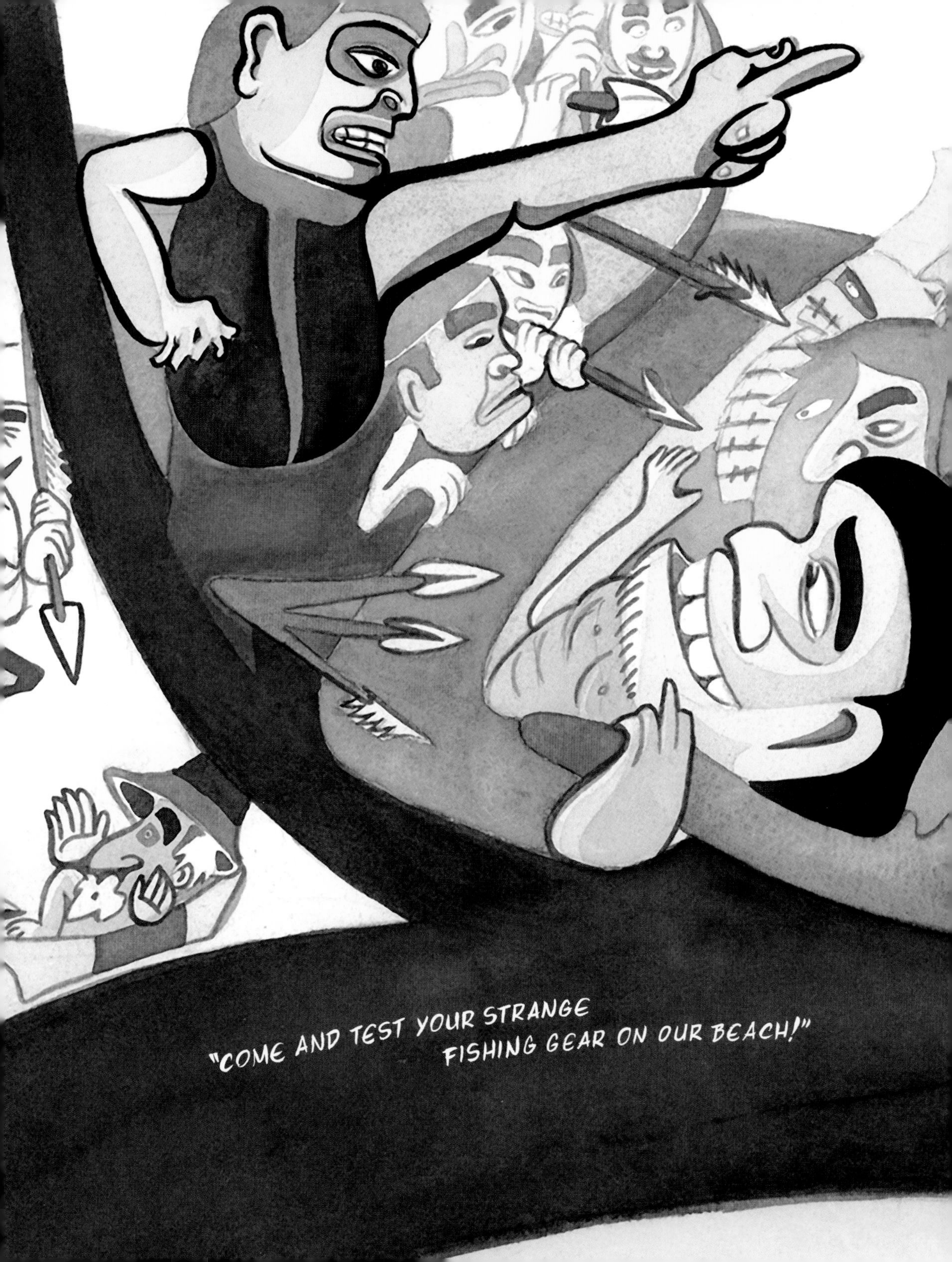
"COME AND TEST YOUR STRANGE
FISHING GEAR ON OUR BEACH!"

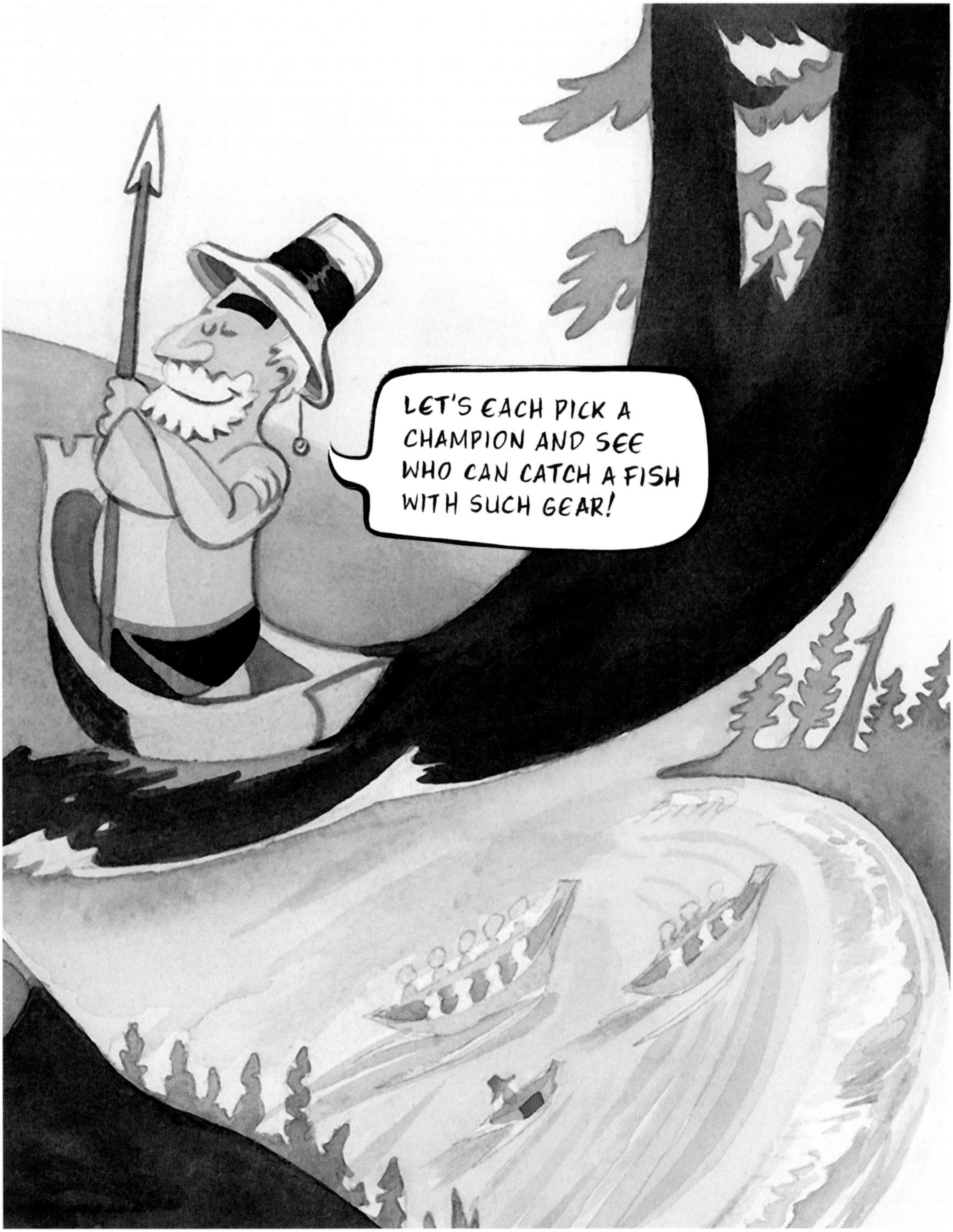
LET'S EACH PICK A CHAMPION AND SEE WHO CAN CATCH A FISH WITH SUCH GEAR!

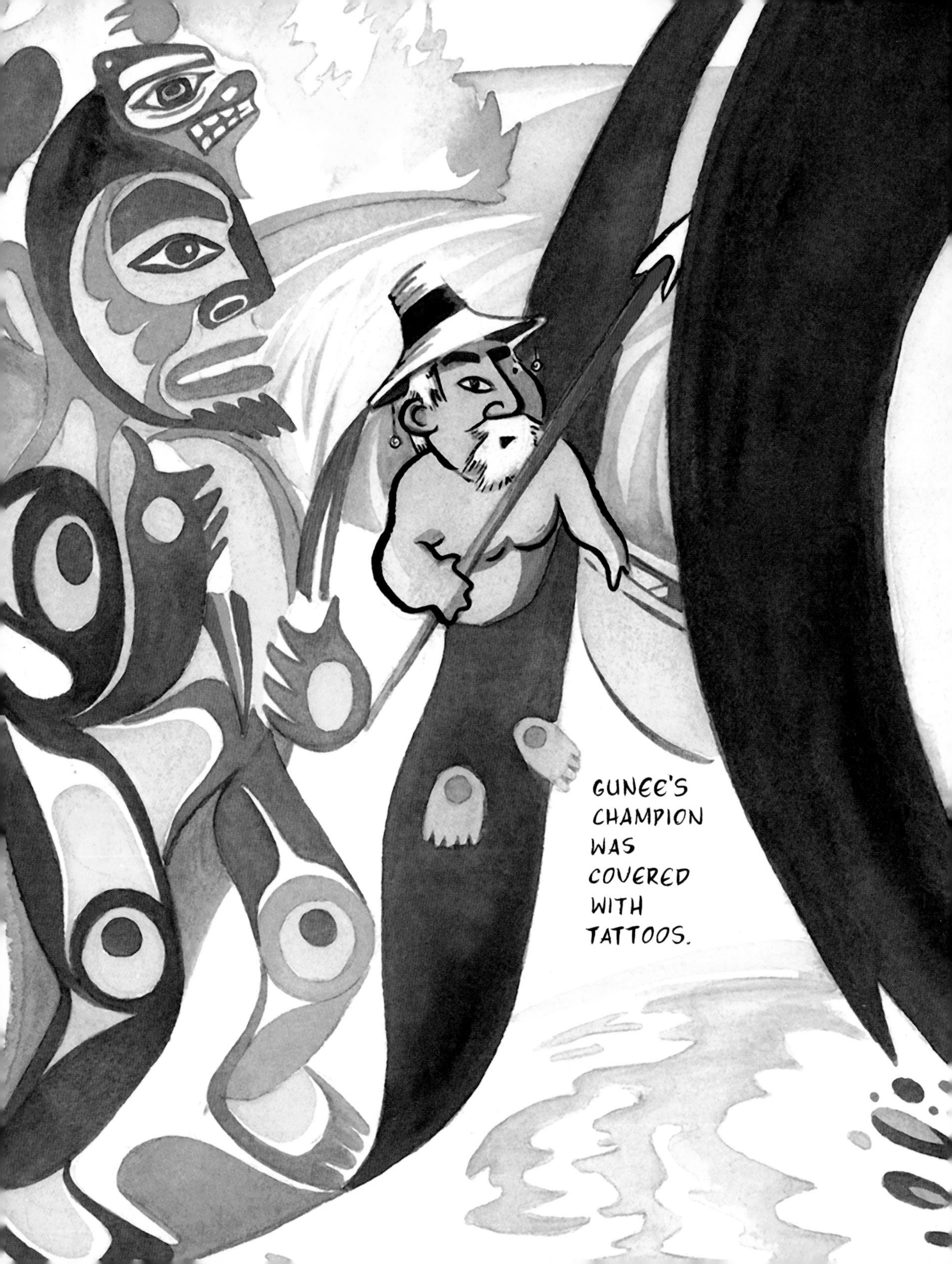
GUNEE'S CHAMPION WAS COVERED WITH TATTOOS.

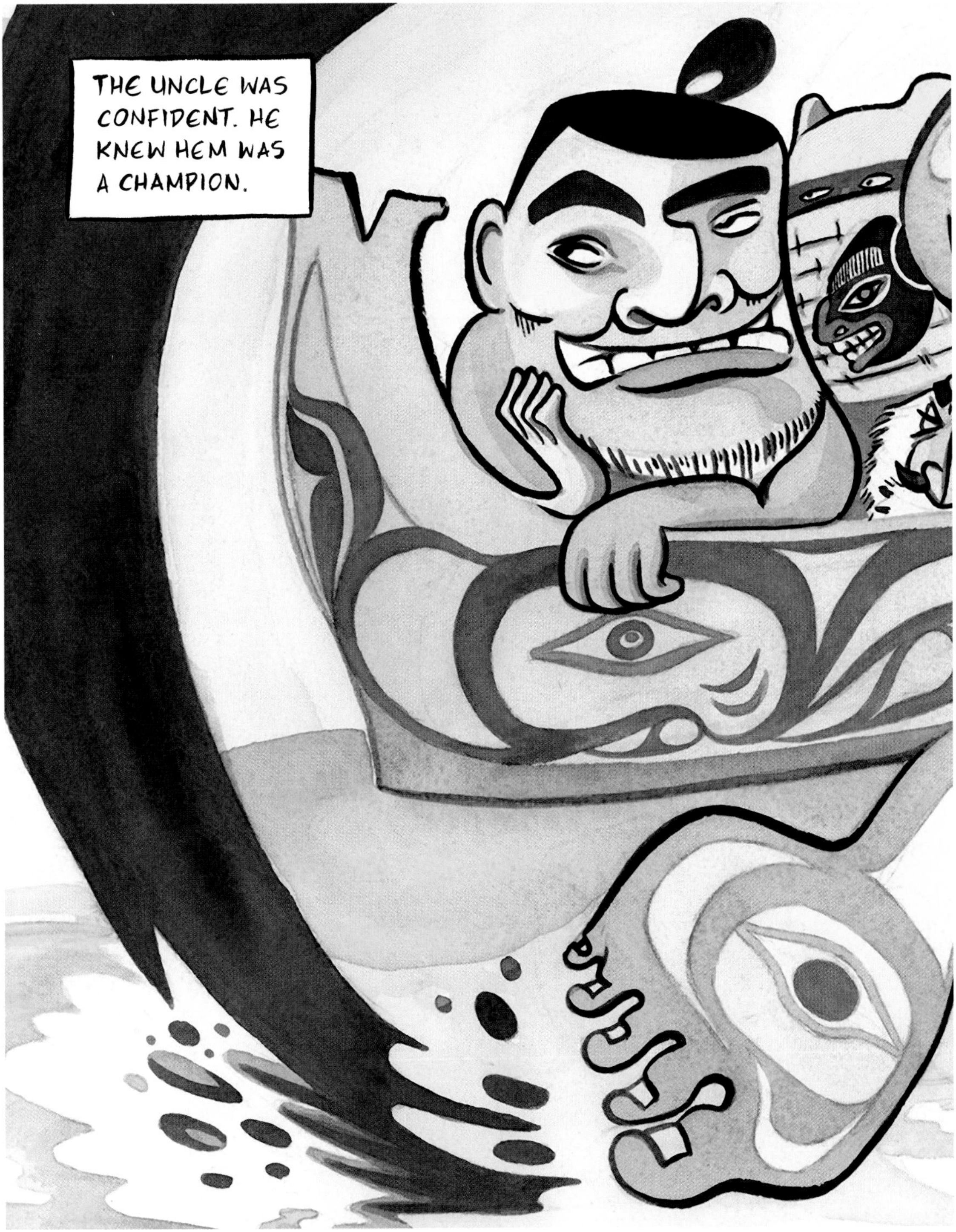
THE UNCLE WAS CONFIDENT. HE KNEW HEM WAS A CHAMPION.

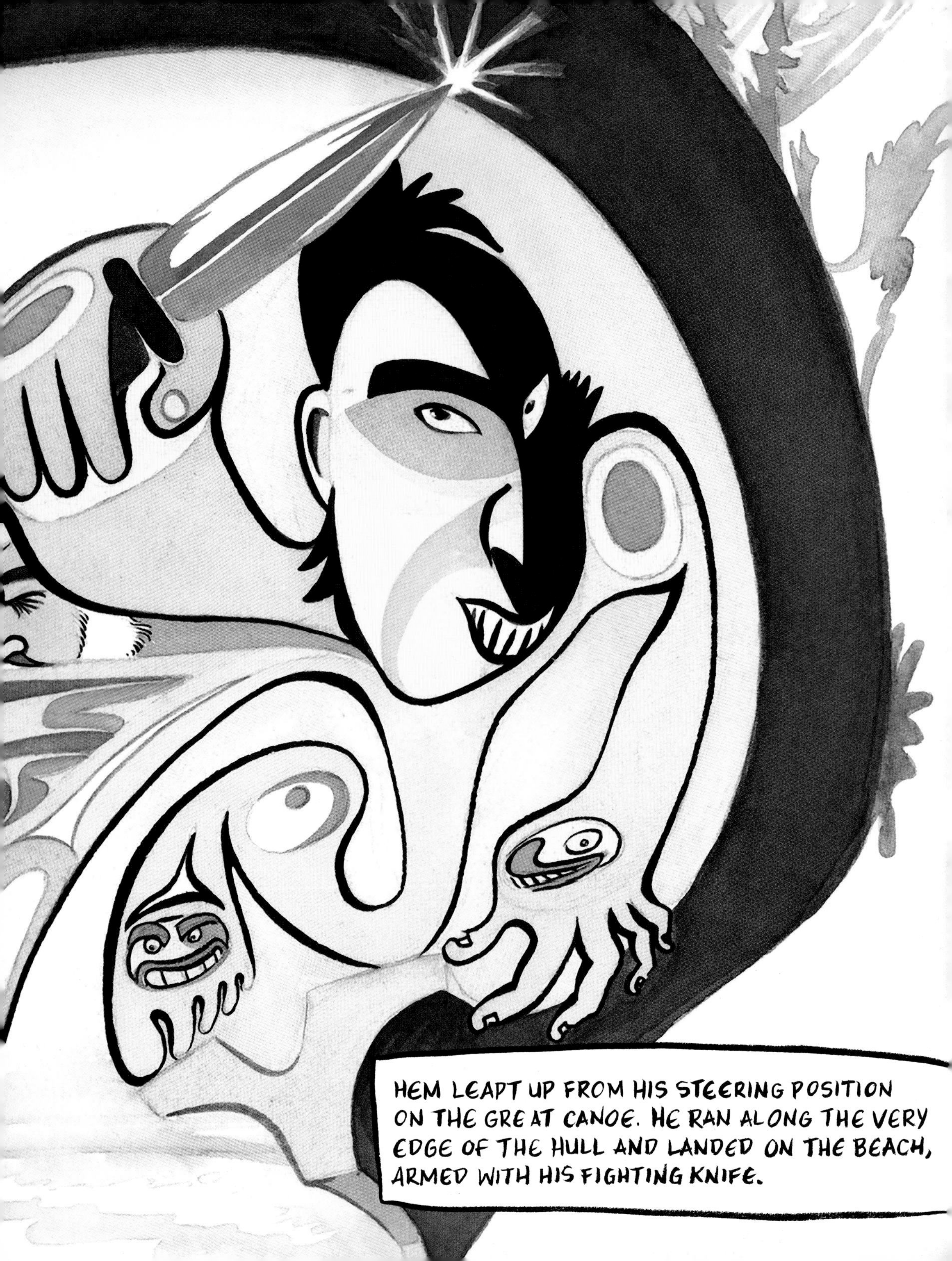
HEM LEAPT UP FROM HIS STEERING POSITION ON THE GREAT CANOE. HE RAN ALONG THE VERY EDGE OF THE HULL AND LANDED ON THE BEACH, ARMED WITH HIS FIGHTING KNIFE.

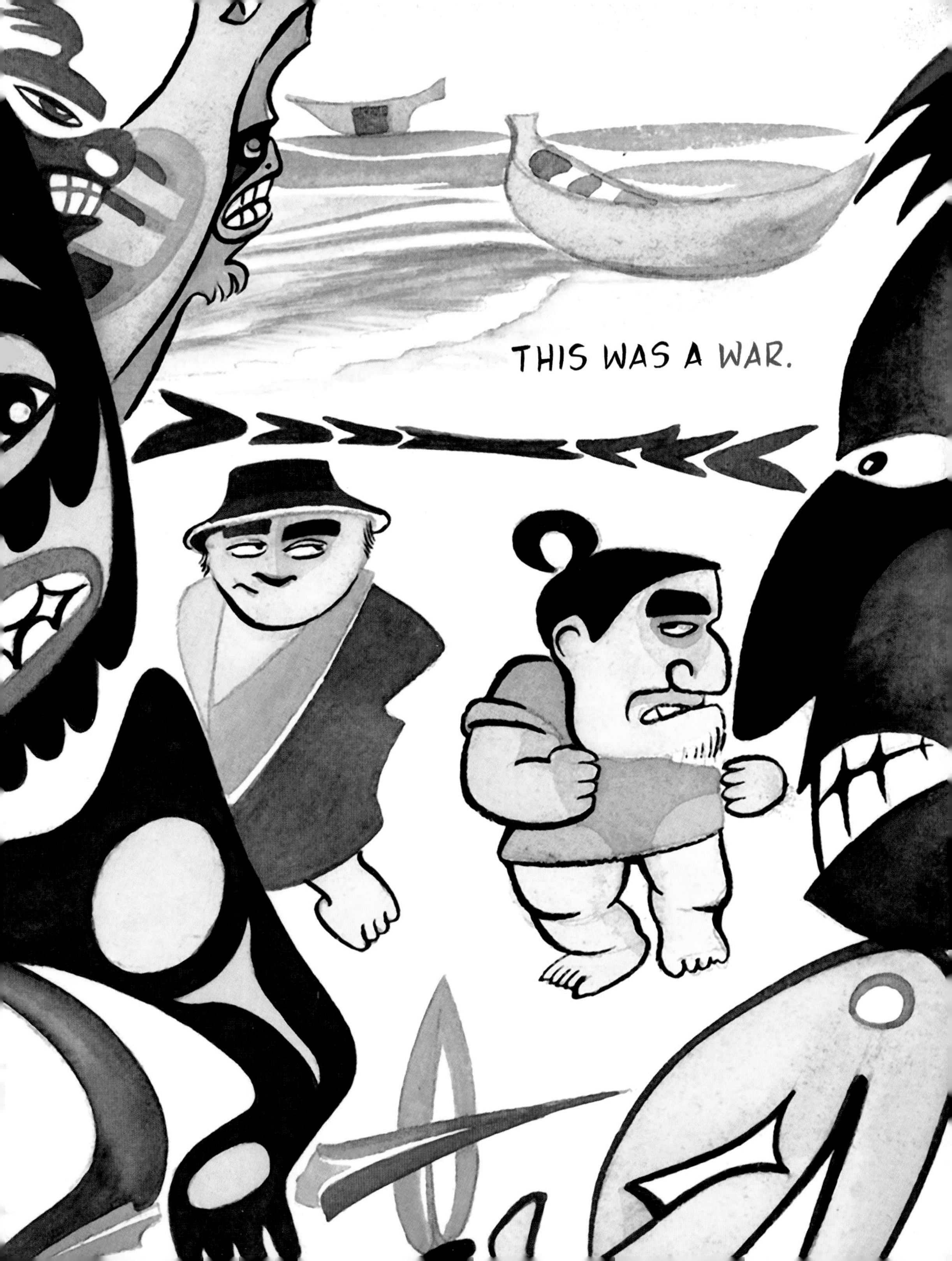
THIS WAS A WAR.

THEY SAY
THAT A
LITTLE
BLOOD WAS
SPILT.

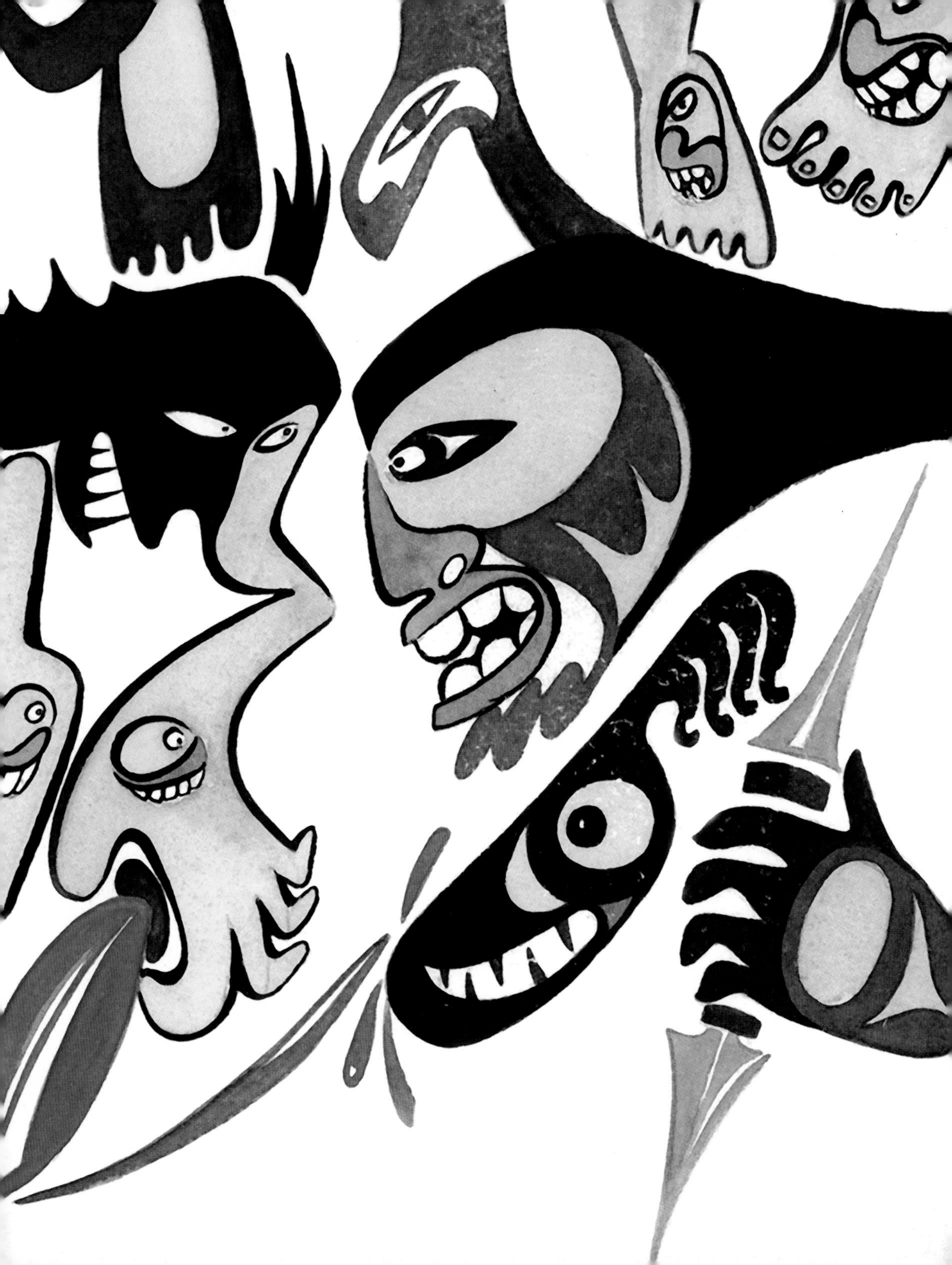

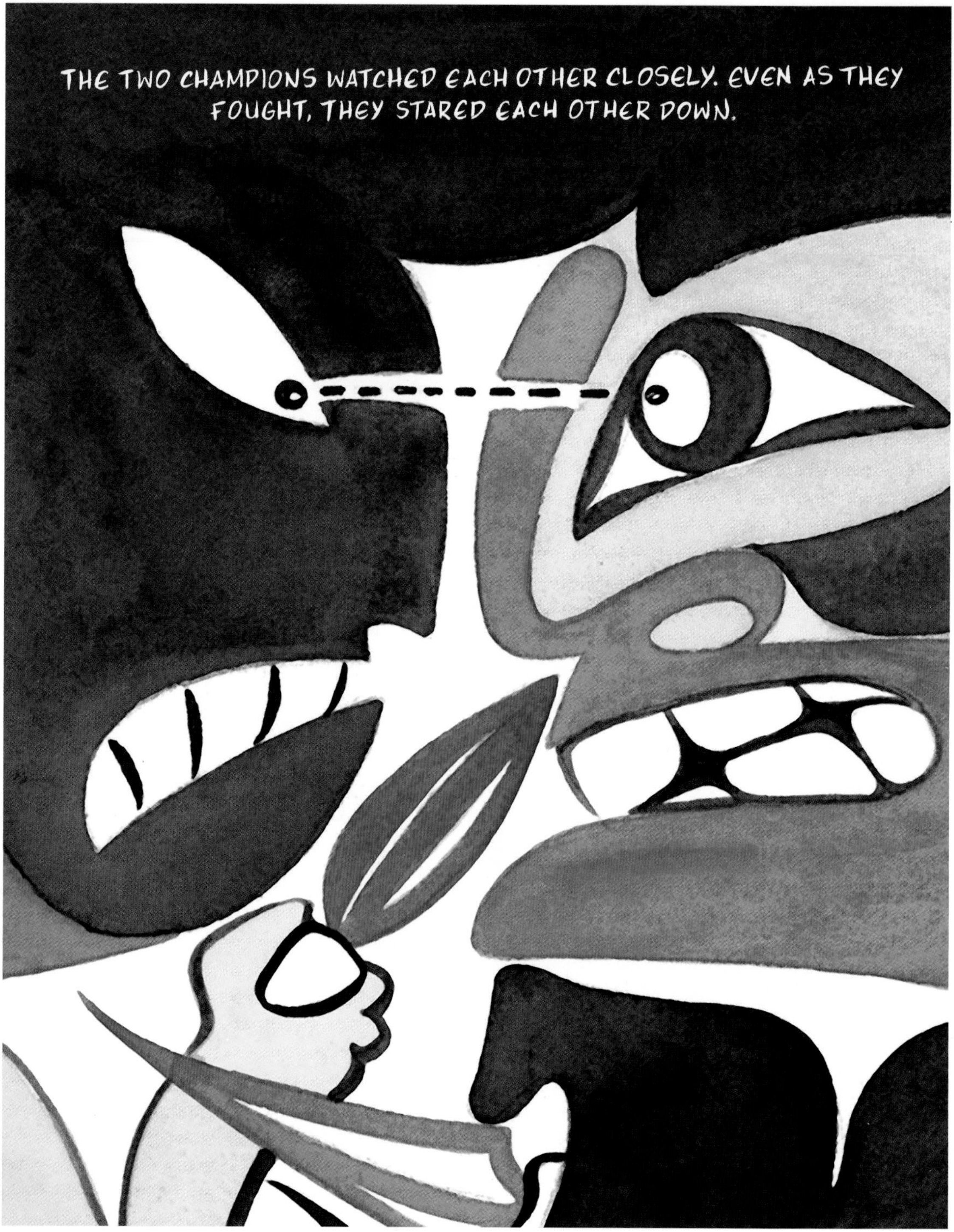
THE TWO CHAMPIONS WATCHED EACH OTHER CLOSELY. EVEN AS THEY FOUGHT, THEY STARED EACH OTHER DOWN.

THAT STRANGE FLY
WAS ALSO THERE.

AND AS THE TWO CHAMPIONS
STARED AND STARED THE FLY
FLEW BY AND ONE OF THEM

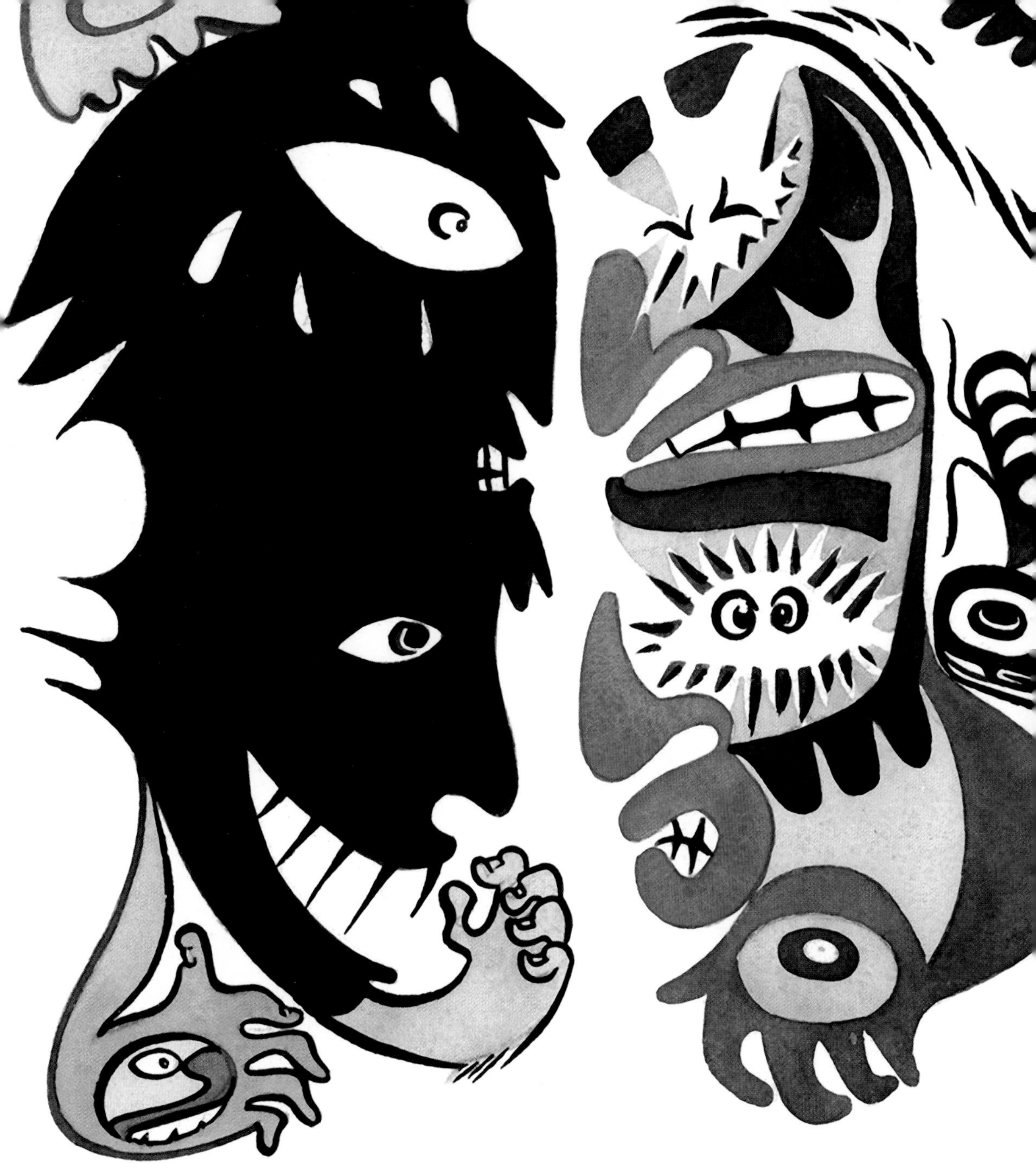

...BLINKED

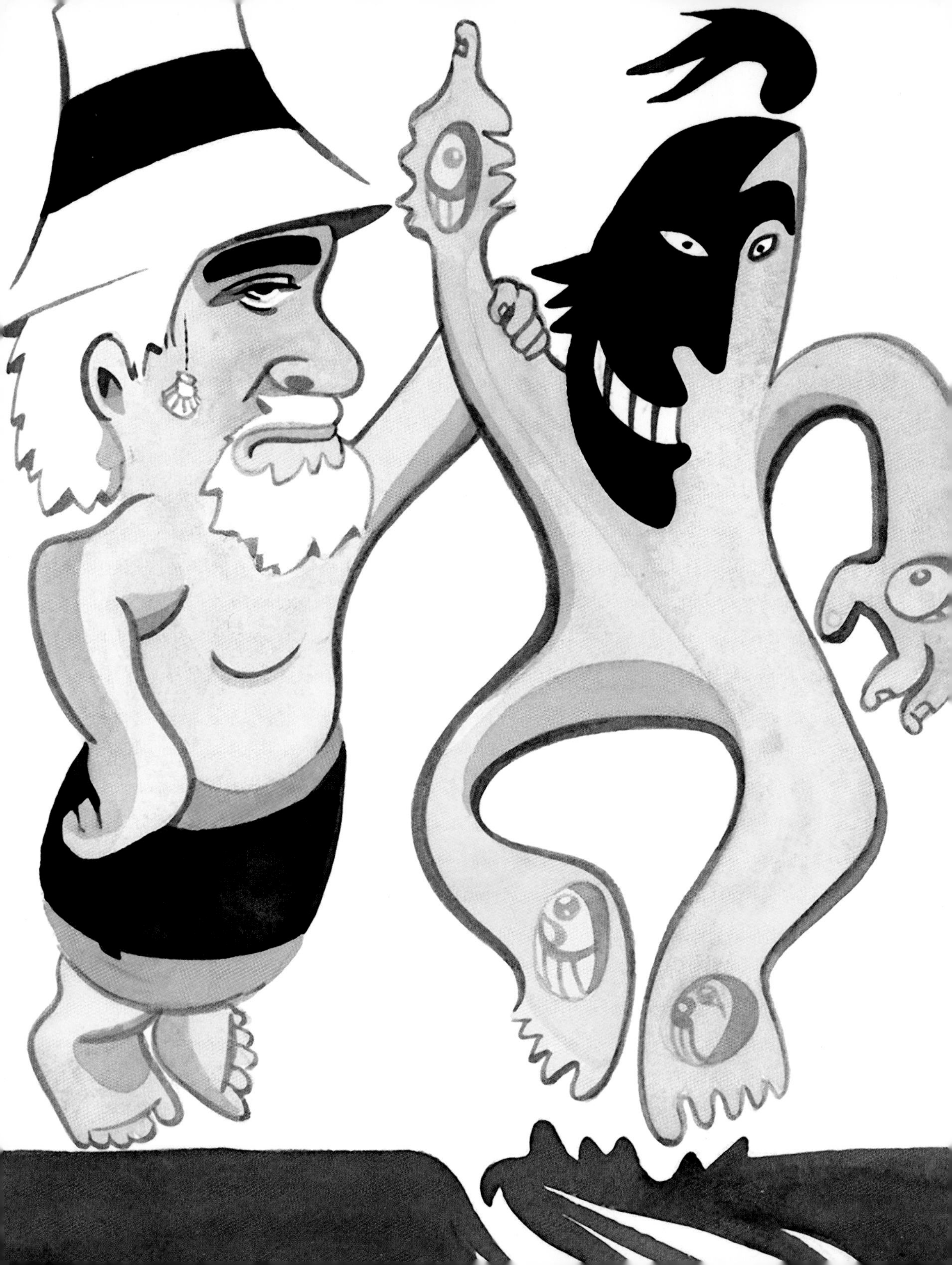

AND BECAUSE HEM'S AND GUNEE'S PEOPLE ARE SUCH GOOD FRIENDS NOW, IT REALLY DOESN'T MATTER WHO BLINKED FIRST.

GUNEE HOSTED A GREAT
DINNER FOR HEM.

EVEN UP TO THIS VERY DAY
THESE PEOPLE STILL HAVE
DINNERS TOGETHER.

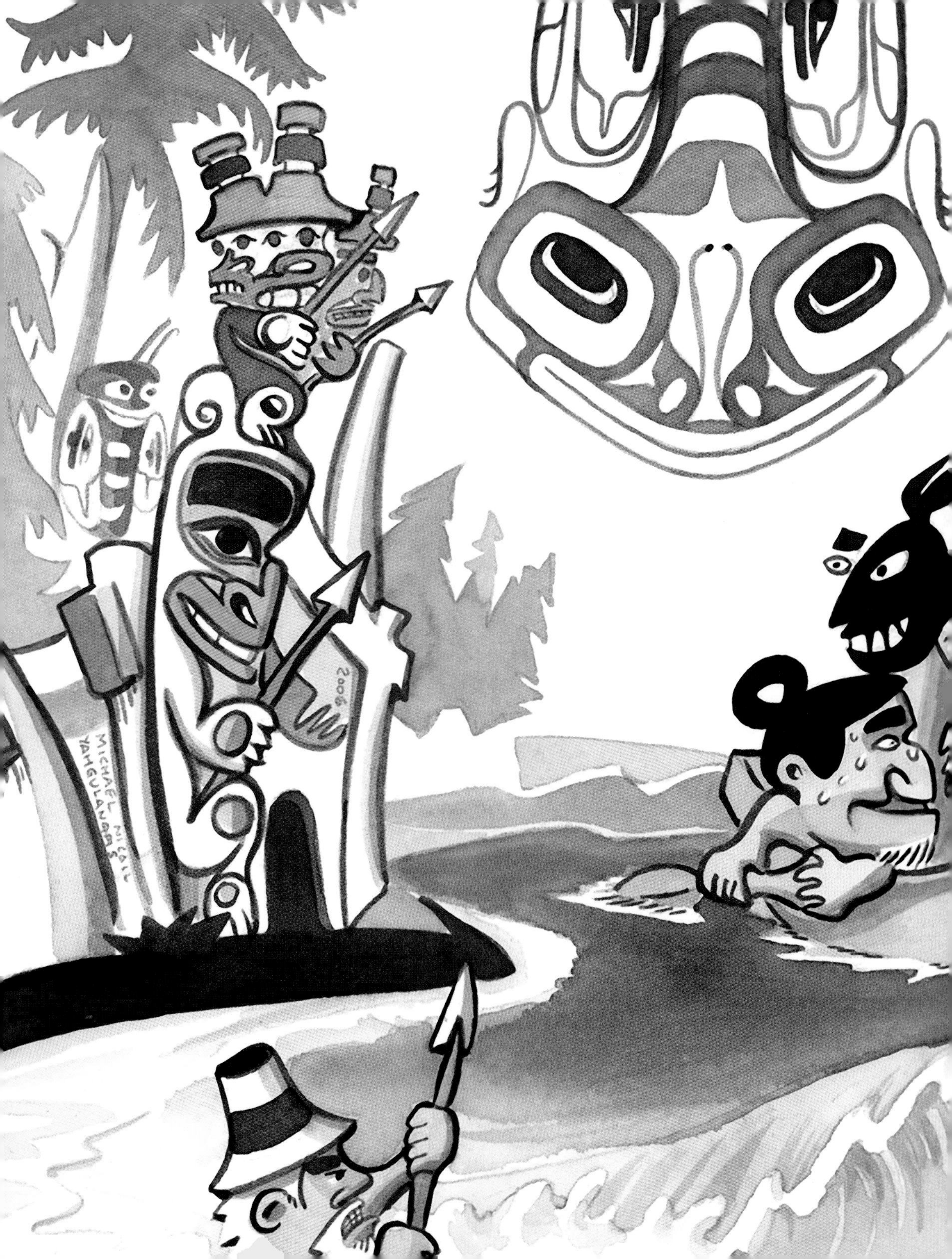
MICHAEL NICOLL
YAHGULANAAS
2006

ABOUT THE AUTHOR

Michael Nicoll Yahgulanaas is the creator of Haida Manga, a distinctive fusion of pop graphics, Haida art and Japanese comic styles. His books include *A Tale of Two Shamans*; *Flight of the Hummingbird*; *Hachidori*, a bestseller in Japan; and *RED: A Haida Manga*, nominated for a BC Book Award, a Doug Wright Award for Best Book, and a 2010 Joe Shuster Award for Outstanding Canadian Cartoonist. *RED* was an Amazon Top 100 book of 2009.

Yahgulanaas is also a sculptor and graphic artist whose work is in the collections of the British Museum, Metropolitan Museum of Art, Seattle Art Museum, Museum of Anthropology, Vancouver Art Gallery, Vancouver International Airport, City of Vancouver, City of Kamloops and University of British Columbia. He pulls from his 20 years of political experience in the Council of the Haida Nation and travels the world speaking to businesses, institutions and communities about social justice, community building, communication and change management. For more, see mny.ca.

Yahgulanaas lives on an island in the Salish Sea, with his wife and daughter.

▶ *War of the Blink*, 66″ × 72″
  watercolour on paper
  private collection

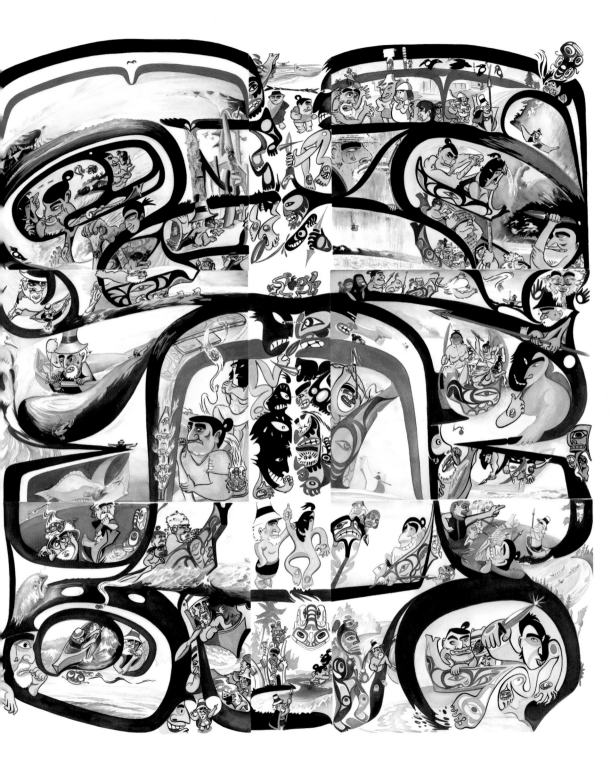

Published in 2017 by Locarno Press,
an imprint of Simply Read Books

locarnopress.com

Artwork and text copyright © 2006,
2017 by Michael Nicoll Yahgulanaas

CIP Data available from Library and Archives Canada

ISBN 978-0-9959946-2-1

We gratefully acknowledge for their financial support of our
publishing program the Canada Council for the Arts, the BC Arts
Council, and the Government of Canada through the Canada
Book Fund (CBF).

Printed in South Korea

10 9 8 7 6 5 4 3 2 1

Art by Michael Nicoll Yahgulanaas and Mirella Nicoll
Hand lettering by Michael Nicoll Yahgulanaas
Cover and interior design by Naomi MacDougall
Edited by Scott Steedman

THANKS

To the MNY Art Inc. studio team, including Mirella Simjuaay Nung Tsuaay Gitans, Launette Marie Rieb and Christopher Waachesday Auchter Yahgulanaas

To Denbigh Fine Art Services

To Nungitlagada Ginowannn Darin Swanson and the Yahgulanaas and Yakjanaas peoples of Auu. To Massett, Skidegate and Kaigani Xaada and their numerous and widespread families. To the team at YPublic Art, particularly Barry Gilson. To the members of the Yahgulanaas Creative Group.

And finally to our neighbours, who became our dear friends during the War of the Blink

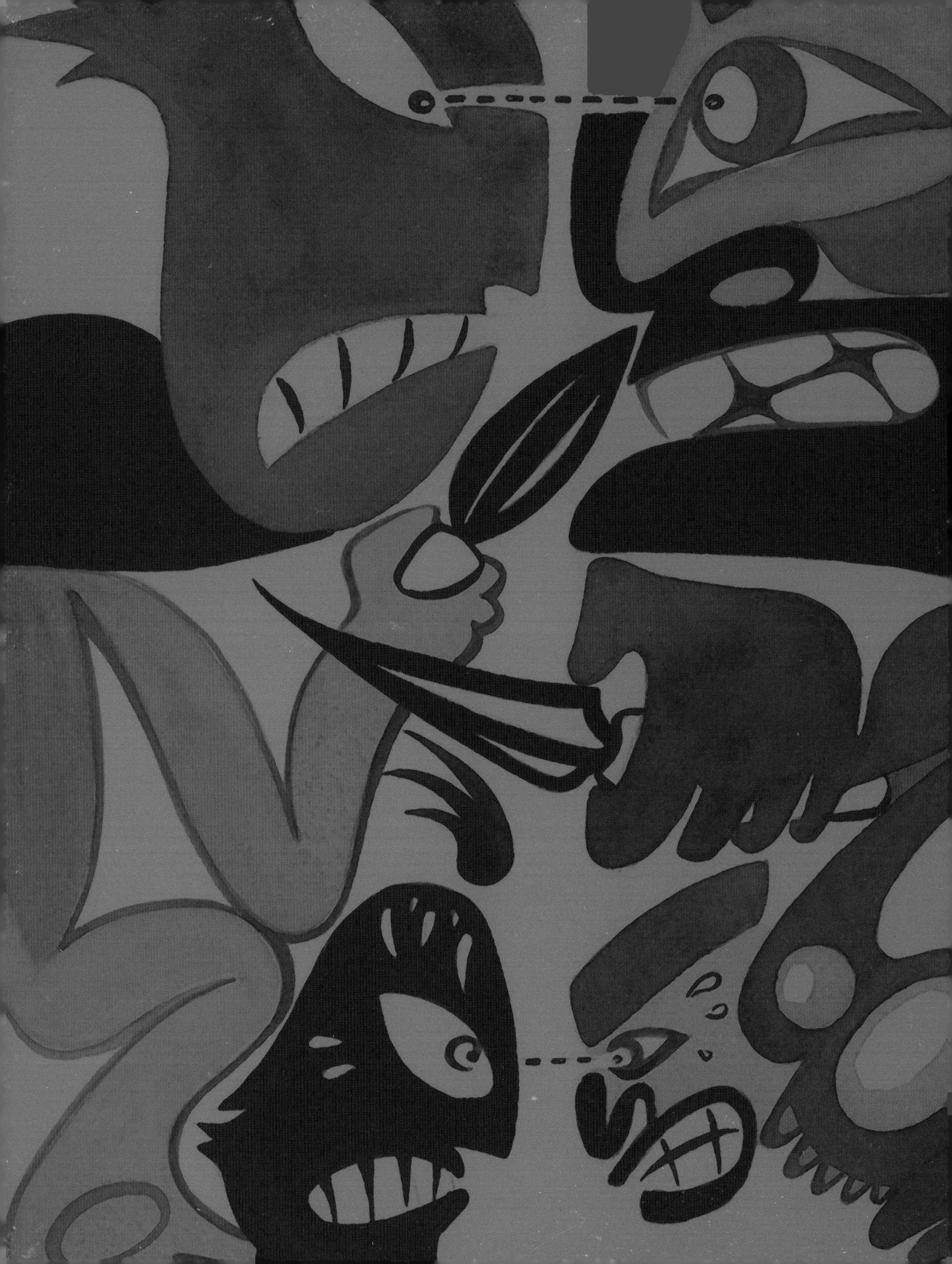